Mission Mover

Thomas G. Bandy

MISSION MOVER

Beyond Education
for Church Leadership

Abingdon Press
Nashville

MISSION MOVER
BEYOND EDUCATION FOR CHURCH LEADERSHIP

Copyright © 2004 by Abingdon Press

All rights reserved.

This book is printed on acid-free paper.

Library of Congress Cataloging-in-Publication Data

Bandy, Thomas G., 1950-
    Mission mover : beyond education for church leadership / by Thomas G. Bandy.
        p. cm.
    ISBN 0-687-33891-3 (pbk. : alk. paper)
1. Christian Leadership.   2. Mission of the church.   I. Title.

BV652.1.B355 2004
253—dc22

                                                                2004003939

All scripture quotations, unless noted otherwise, are taken from the *New Revised Standard Version of the Bible,* copyright © 1989, by the Division of Christian Education of the National Council of the Churches of Christ in the United States of America. Used by permission. All rights reserved.

04 05 06 07 08 09 10 11 12 13—10 9 8 7 6 5 4 3 2 1

MANUFACTURED IN THE UNITED STATES OF AMERICA

This book is dedicated to all those Christian leaders

in North America and around the world

who have staked everything

(pension plan, family security, affluence, and influence)

to walk with Jesus into mission

CONTENTS

FOREWORD

Tom Bandy has written many important books. Each was written with passion, courage, brilliance, and practicality.

But in my opinion, Tom Bandy has never written anything as important, passionate, brilliant, incisive, practical, courageous, and revolutionary as the book you are now holding.

In fact, in my opinion, very few people have written anything on Christian leadership and mission comparable in importance to *Mission Mover* in a long time. That's not hyperbole. That's my honest assessment of the book you're now holding. To make my point a little more bluntly:

- If a seminary president in the English-speaking world refuses to read and ponder this book and take its message seriously, I think he or she should be gently but firmly replaced. If he says he is too busy to read it or simply lacks time due to other pressing demands, he should be given a week of paid study leave, as soon as possible, to prayerfully read this book and report on it to his board, who should also read it with prayer and concern. Board meeting agendas should be revised to allow a day, at least, to dialogue about this book and what it means.
- If seminary professors don't read and discuss this book on faculty retreats and over cups of coffee and long

lunches, if denominational officials (conservative or liberal, Catholic or Protestant or Orthodox, Third World or Western World or Whatever World) don't engage in heated and serious dialogue about it, donors should withhold their funds until they do. (If oncologists didn't keep up with the latest cancer research, wouldn't we call it criminal for them to continue practicing medicine? Lives would be at stake! Is less at stake here?)

- If potential seminary students don't read this book before they pay their first tuition dollar (or incur their first tuition debt), they're naïve or lazy, not the kind of students we need entering paid ministry in the years ahead. If they do read this book, they may decide to invest their tuition dollars very differently. At the very least, they'll make new demands on their seminaries—demands that over a decade or so could radically alter how seminaries work.

- If local church pastors don't allow this book to challenge their thinking on the purpose of the church in today's and tomorrow's worlds, then ... then I hope they have a nice day. And I also hope that people with vision will migrate toward other churches, those with leaders who do grapple with the missional questions raised here.

The book won't make anyone happy. It's troubling. It will ruffle feathers, cause backsides that are comfortable in soft office chairs to squirm, and stir up lots of arguments. But the arguments stirred up by this book are worth having, unlike most of the arguments we're currently having. If church boards and church leaders do read this book and take its message seriously, they will be tempted toward revolutionary thinking—exactly the kind of thinking we need.

I'm tempted to list, in advance, the kind of excuses people will make—the reasons they'll give for calling Tom Bandy impractical, overly critical, unpolitical, blah, blah, blah—so they can dismiss this book and get back to business as usual. But I can't stomach that exercise.

Yes, sadly, a lot of people will blissfully evade the message of this book. I just hope you won't be one of them.

A few years ago, I was kindly invited to speak to the Fellowship of Evangelical Seminary Presidents. After my lectures on the post-modern transition and what it means for Christian leadership development, one seminary president pulled me aside and said something like this:

> I hope you don't think we can actually *do anything* about this. I hope you're not that naïve. Our students don't come to be edu-cated and stretched. They come to be certified as quickly as possible. The churches that send them don't want them to be challenged to think anything new; they want them to be given ammunition to defend what they already knew when they came. The seminary donors and board members don't want to change the world; they want to save their institutions with min-imum pain, inconvenience, and cost. The denominational structures don't want students to be trained *how to think*; that's too risky. They just want them to be indoctrinated in *what to think*. And the accrediting structures—don't even let me get started on them. They're perfectly designed to mass-produce educational mediocrity.

I replied, "Yes, it's a systems thing, isn't it. The current inter-locking systems of denominations, seminaries, religious broad-casting, publishing, mission agencies, Sunday school curriculum producers, religious music producers, and all the rest perfectly conspire to maintain the status quo. Change in any one sector of the system is punished and absorbed by the other sectors of the system."

He thought for a second, nodded thoughtfully, and then added, "I guess the only way to change the system is to have revolution in every sector, all at the same time. How likely is that?"

It's highly unlikely, but for people who believe in a God for whom nothing is impossible, "unlikely" shouldn't be a major problem. What Tom Bandy presents in this book can inspire that kind of system-wide revolution—if you and I take it seriously, talk about it, disseminate it, stir the pot, take some risks, have some hope, exercise some faith.

Revolution is dangerous, you say.

Yes, but the status quo is even more dangerous—more dangerous because it's comfortable and familiar—and profitable for too many of us.

A lot is at stake in how this book is marketed, distributed, read, and discussed. I hope these few words will engender in you a sense of seriousness as you prepare to turn the next page. Prayerful seriousness. And wild hope too.

Because these pages could help inspire a revolution that is so stinking exciting I can hardly stand thinking about it.

Brian McLaren
Pastor, author
(anewkindofchristian.com, emergentvillage.com)

WELCOME: YOU HAVE MAIL!

Welcome to my e-mail correspondence! This book is a summary of correspondence over the past several years with a large and diverse group of Christians who share only one thing in common: the uneasy feeling that God is calling them into ministry. They share little else. Some have church backgrounds and some do not: men and women; old people, young people, and ageless people; Caucasian, African-American, Asian, Native American; high school graduates and high school dropouts; extroverts and introverts; people with every reason to love the church and people with every reason to despise the church.

I have conflated, arranged, and edited the correspondence as if it is with one person, but it is a real correspondence and captures the real questions and issues that surface again and again. I have left it in e-mail form because that is how people today are accustomed to format their learning. Gone are the tidy chapters, linear outlines, didactic sermons, lengthy essays, and extended bibliographies. The e-mail format will make this book harder to read and easier to dismiss by seminary professors and classically trained clergy—and easier to read and harder to put down by everybody else. And there, in a nutshell, is the rationale for the book. The denominational certification and seminary education that has dominated the church for over five centuries is missing the mark largely because denominations and seminaries are aiming at the wrong thing. It is about time the church recognized the opportunity and stopped lamenting the catastrophe.

My e-mail correspondence (and personal conversation, observation, and experience over twenty-five years of ordained leadership in three denominations and two countries) has forced upon me an unsettling conclusion. Nobody wants to be educated for church leadership, because in his or her deepest heart nobody wants to lead a church. At least, not a "church" as it has come to be defined over the past several hundred years. Instead, increasing numbers of people, often at the margins of traditional "churchy" life, are eager to immerse themselves in a missional movement that has Christ at the center of the mayhem.

People aspiring to be "church leaders" are obsessed by certifications, salary packages, career paths, standardized policies and Mondays off. People aspiring to be mission movers are willing to merge their entire lifestyle with the mission and say to heck with the details. The former are willing to wait 3-4 years for training, pay their dues for another 3-4 years working among people who were never their primary concern in the first place, and eventually settle down in the locality where they always wanted to be, hoping that no bishop will move them and no conflict will crush them. The latter are going to start tomorrow, among the specific people for whom their heart bursts, and all they require is the confidence that they can learn what they need when they need it. Their tenacity will defeat any bishop trying to move them, and their passion for personal growth and pragmatic adaptability will get around any conflict or obstacle the devil puts in their path.

This is why the investment of the Lilly Foundation and other funding organizations to develop innovative programs for "education for church leadership" is so futile. As a consultant, I myself have worked with educational centers, judicatories, and nonprofit organizations to develop grant proposals or apply newly funded strategies to recruit, train, and deploy "ministers." What has impressed me most about these proposals and programs is their singular lack of imagination and their general inability to think beyond the box of traditional processes of education and polity. Yet the leaders involved are intelligent and creative people. Why are the resulting proposals and programs so dull? The answer is that the very goal to "educate for church leadership" is misdirected. Simply stated, in the post-Christendom, postmodern spiritual ferment of the emerging pagan world, nobody really wants to lead a church in the first place. There are many people who *are* willing to risk their families, reduce their incomes, lose their friends, jeopardize their safety, go into debt for training, and destabilize their lives *for something worthwhile*. But the "church" is not it. Christ is it. Mission is it. But the institutional church is not it.

This e-mail correspondence explores the implications of this reality. Prior to publication, I presented this correspondence in dramatic fashion in the regional Convergence events sponsored by *Easum, Bandy and Associates*. In these regional events, the EBA team, pastors, and volunteers from across the denominational and theological spectrum "converge" for illumination, practical training, and networking. My presentation (dramatized with the help of EBA Associate Linnea Nilsen Capshaw) never failed to be controversial. I remember one small group debriefing during the presentation. Out of a group of about nine people, three "traditional" pastors were so mad that they left the building. Three other leaders were so mad at these pastors for refusing to face the truth, that they left the building. And the three remaining leaders tried desperately to keep them in the room, arguing that "Bandy is just exaggerating in order to make a point." They failed, of course, because the truth is that Bandy was not exaggerating at all. He was just describing the real reasons why the North American church is facing an escalating shortage of church leaders, and why all the millions of dollars of foundation money to promote education for church leadership will be revealed to be futile in ten years. He was also describing an alternative that would immerse people in mission movement, which, if equally funded, could change the course of Christian mission in North America today. Unfortunately, it is an alternative that would turn seminary curricula and denominational polity upside down and endanger professorial tenure and judicatory control.

In order to make sense of this, you need to understand a few things about my e-mail.

First, as an author, speaker, consultant, and coach, I read and respond to about fifty to one hundred e-mail messages a day. Some are addressed to me through the website and forums of *Easum, Bandy and Associates* at www.easumbandy.com. Some are forwarded to me from my e-mail address for *Net Results* magazine: tgbandy@netresults.org. Most comes directly to me at tgbandy@aol.com.

Second, I approach e-mail in general, and specific postings in particular, in a matrix of prayer and meditation. It is part of my daily spiritual discipline. It is not just that I try to respond with as much intelligence as I can muster, but that I try to respond with as much focus on mission as possible. Therefore, my e-mail is not really a form of personal sharing, but a form of substantive dialogue. It resembles a high-speed version of apostolic epistle writing.

Third, I am known for long e-mail messages. Whether it is a passion for clarity, or a knack for fast typing, most people quickly recognize that e-mail for me is *not* a vehicle for idle chatter. I don't do chat rooms. I do conversation. I don't do long-distance pastoral care. I do coaching. I am not interested in the weather where somebody lives, but in the growth of their soul and the state of their mission.

Participants in online forums and seminars relish sending tidbits and half-baked ideas along with a disclaimer that these are their "two cents." Stupid, ill-considered, and merely sentimental posts clutter the Internet like advertising on the highway. I abhor any e-mail that is worth only "two cents" in the estimation of the sender. This is not to say that I don't occasionally receive (and even personally send) messages that are regrettable or that prove to be worth far less than originally thought. At the time of sending, however, good e-mail should be worth "a million dollars" (or at least a hundred) in the estimation of the sender. Only the devil inspires junk mail.

All this is to say that this collection of e-mail may be occasionally wrong, but it is all *worthwhile*. In the same Convergence events where this correspondence was dramatically presented, there were always men and women in tears telling me that I had articulated their yearning and their frustration. I had shown them why they were so passionate about mission, so unhappy in their seminary course, and so frustrated with their judicatory. And yes, at the end of the presentation there were always a handful of seminary teachers and judicatory leaders brimming with excitement because at last they understood why their highly funded, intelligent creativity was bearing so little fruit ... and what they could do about it.

There is hope.

Tom Bandy
Day 247+ on the Road to Mission
2003

1

I REMEMBER YOU!

E-mail #1
Subject: Sure, I Remember You

Dear Friend:

Thanks for your message. You write: "You may not remember me from the workshop last week, but I was the one to ask you during the break whether you thought ordination was important or not for someone thinking about the ministry. I've been lurking on the listserv for some time, and praying about it. I'm a female, fairly conservative, broadly intellectual, introverted person who already has a good job, a promising career, and lots of friends. But this idea of ministry just won't let go of me, and most of my friends think I am nuts. What do I do?"

Thirty-five years ago when there was still a secular world, fewer and fewer people inquired about Christian ministry because, after all, God was supposed to be dead. And seminary enrollments declined. Today, in this bubbling cauldron of spiritual ferment, lots of people inquire about Christian ministry . . . but fewer and fewer of them decide to pursue it, because God is alive and well everywhere in the world except the institutional church. And seminary enrollments decline.

Yesterday's challenge was to find leaders to help people discern God in the midst of godlessness. Today's challenge is to find leaders to help people discern Christ in the midst of godliness. Can you do that? Are you excited about that?

The fundamental question you need to ask and answer is: *Do you really, really want to be with Jesus on the road to mission?* How you answer this question will largely determine your future. Unfortunately, how your pastor who was ordained 35 years ago answered this question, and how you need to answer this question, is different. That's one big reason why you are confused and trading e-mail with me, instead of eagerly talking to your pastor.

E-mail #2
Subject: The Hidden Dread

Dear Confused Christian:

Thanks for your honesty in these comments: "You're right. I don't really know who to talk to, and although I like my pastor a lot, he can't seem to help me in this decision. When I shared my interest with my pastor, he asked me what my position was on the inerrancy of Scripture and abortion. I talked to my bishop, and he commented that I might make a great youth worker. I talked to the dean of the nearby seminary, and he suggested I sign up right away for clinical pastoral education. Yesterday the church nominations committee phoned to say they had heard I was a student for ordination, and would I be interested in joining the official board and serving on the pastoral visitation committee. Yesterday I was filled with enthusiasm, and today I am filled with dread! Oh by the way ... I also talked to my Christian friend who owns a Mail Boxes Etc. franchise, and she offered me a job. What's going on here?"

That "dread" is the real reason no serious missionary wants to be educated for church leadership. It's the same problem faced by the earliest church in Acts. You want to be on the open road, way, way beyond Emmaus, and the head office in Jerusalem wants you to take residence in the Upper Room to service the infrastructure, serve potluck suppers, and take care of the members until they die. You're a roadrunner, and they want innkeepers.

You must understand from the beginning, my Christian friend, that there is a fundamental disconnect between your calling and the expectations of the church. The institutional leaders who decide and shape denominational and seminary processes simply do not understand you. They are nice people. They are faithful Christians. But they do not understand you. They do not understand the sense of calling that God has elicited from the new generation of Christian leaders today.

- They do not really understand you and your generation of leaders, and therefore they struggle to interface their hoops and hurdles for denominational certification with your needs and expectations. They struggle to design a learning content and methodology that will truly be useful to you in real ministry in the twenty-first century.
- And because they struggle to interface a process and design a program with this new generation of Christian leaders, you will almost inevitably face future dilemmas about whether to stay with the seminary course or blaze your own learning path, and whether to stay with the denomination or plant your own independent church.

It is inevitable. I am sorry to say it. It will impose a stress on your life beyond the already significant stress of rejection by your peers, pressure from pagan society, and the anxiety of your spouse and children. This fundamental lack of understanding for your call within the judicatory and seminary is often a splash of cold water that ultimately dampens enthusiasm and turns potential Christian leaders away from the church. Yet I hope, if you are aware of this disconnect from the very beginning, you will be able to customize a process for yourself using denominational, seminary, and other resources that will equip you for the real calling you actually experience.

E-mail #3
Subject: The Great Disconnect

Dear Confused Christian:
Here is the disconnect between your calling and institutional expectations that you must understand. Denominations and seminaries still believe that the goal is "education for church leadership"! I know, I know, it is amazing. One wonders how professionals and scholars who talk so much about the postmodern world can fail so utterly to understand the implications of it, but there it is. These people still believe that "education for church leadership" matters.

Over the past decade, the Lilly Foundation has given millions of dollars to institutions to develop innovative programs to educate church leaders in recognition of the serious shortage of clergy. I have reviewed many of these programs . . . even consulted with institutions to develop proposals. Most of the ideas are anything but innovative: open houses or short-term experiences in seminaries; vocational coaching in camp ministries; curriculums for church youth groups; web networks to compare job opportunities. The lack of imagination over tactics is indicative of the deeper problem. These are all "churchy" tactics designed to persuade candidates to be educated for *church leadership*.

The problem is that healthy, intelligent, innovative, deeply spiritual, passionately faithful Christians today *will have nothing to do with church leadership*! No one wants to preserve an institution. No one wants to endure the backbiting, and perpetual fundraising, and constant whining for personal attention from an aging remnant.

- No one wants to maintain a dogged allegiance to outmoded organizational practices, or cherish inefficient facilities, or walk people liturgically through a supposedly Christian calendar that has no impact whatsoever on the course of human history.
- No one wants to invest their lives in useless denominational policy development, or constantly compare

themselves for better or worse to whatever is considered theologically pure or politically correct, or compete with career colleagues in the quest for a "better" church (i.e., a bigger, happier, more financially stable church).

- No one wants to spend their lives justifying their salaried existence, all the while watching Christian friends in business, health care, social service, non-profit charity, and even corporate industry do great stuff, raise healthy families, pay for the children's university education without overwhelming debt, and glorify God along the way.

- And most of all—*truly of most importance*—is that no one is willing to be crucified for their refusal to do any of the above things. They are willing to be crucified for their Lord, but they are *not willing* to be crucified for their church.

Fewer and fewer people really want to be educated for church leadership. You don't want to be educated for church leadership. To be honest, I do not think God wants you to be educated for church leadership.

What you do want—what a whole new generation of called Christians wants—and what God wants is *education for mission immersion*. This is what the denominational and seminary planners have yet to comprehend, and until they do—and change—no amount of foundation money is going to increase the supply of clergy in North America.

Education for mission immersion means growing and equipping the teams of spiritual entrepreneurs who will risk anything, do anything, change anything, in order to help people experience the transforming power of God and be encouraged to walk with Jesus into mission themselves. The focus is not even on "leadership," but on mission. It is not about who does it, who certifies it, who controls it ... but about sharing it, living it, and releasing it irresistibly and uncontrollably in every emerging micro-culture. It is not about how to grow a church, take care of church members, and repeat sacred acts in continuity with a heritage … but about reaching out, discipling strangers, and inventing new sacred acts in continuity with Christ's creativity.

Mission immersion is about throwing yourself headlong into the micro-culture for whom your heart bursts. It's about spending your life savings to set sail from Troas, taking a straight shot to Samothrace, not pausing to gape at the Winged Victory but pressing on to Neapolis, and ending up in Philippi … where you immediately learn their dialect, come to appreciate odd-tasting foods, dress in different ways, listen to weird music, and adapt your entire lifestyle to that of the Macedonians … for the sole purpose of helping them experience Jesus. And when you are done, you will move on to Thessalonica and cause the same uproar there.

Mission immersion is different from church leadership. It is like the mission to the gentiles of the first apostolic age. It is all about learning the trade of being a Christian leader in a cross-disciplinary, cross-cultural, cross-experiential world that is a bubbling cauldron of spiritual ferment in which Christianity is just one small potato.

The denomination and seminary talk about the postmodern world, but still behave as if sacred mission can only come from a sacred people who live in a sacred facility and worship at sacred times. But you instinctively understand that sacred mission comes first. It is sacred mission that will make any people, any property, and any time sacred. Every minority, every affinity group, every food court or barroom, every lifestyle moment can be sacred if only God seizes it, and you want to be a part of it.

Fundamentally, your complete disinterest in "education for church leadership" and your wholehearted passion for "education for mission immersion" are what seminary and denominational leaders do not understand. You will always remain a bit of a mystery to them … and perhaps a serious threat … unless they awaken to the implications of "being church" in the emerging pagan, postmodern world.

E-mail #4
Subject: The Three Key Questions

Dear Confused Christian (Warning: This is a long post):

So you tell me that you are seriously considering devoting your life to Christian ministry. As a Christian, you are already devoted to Christian mission, since the call to multiply disciples is implied by the very experience of baptism. If you are not already deeply involved in some form of hands-on, personal mission through which you simultaneously bless other people beyond your family or tribe *and* readily articulate your faith motivation for doing it, then please stop reading immediately. Delete this e-mail from your mailbox.

Christian ministry means leadership of Christian people to share the gospel among pagan publics. It is not a venue for seekers to "find themselves" or for philanthropists to do "good service." This leadership assumes that you have already had an experience with Jesus Christ that has transformed your life for the good and compelled you to share it with other people. This leadership assumes that you are convinced that the experience of Christ is the ultimate expression of love in which other people can experience physical, emotional, intellectual, relational, and spiritual *abundant life*. No doubt this leadership will cause you to nurture the fellowship of Christ (a companionship that is sometimes, but not always, referred to as "the church"), but only insofar as that fellowship of Christ is motivated and equipped for mission among pagan publics. No doubt this leadership will cause you to lead positive personal, social, local, and global change, but only insofar as that change is clearly motivated by—and fulfilled in—relationship to Christ. If these things are not on the horizon of your heart, rest assured that you are still a very good person. You can give wonderful service to humanity, and find excellent training from many sources, and lead a very fulfilling life, but please do not consider devoting your life to Christian ministry. Christian ministry means leadership of Christian people to share the gospel among pagan publics.

There are three basic questions that you need to consider if you are devoting your life to Christian ministry.

First, *do you really want to do this to yourself*? I phrase the question this way because the challenge you face is not so much the devotion of your *life* to Christian ministry as the devotion of your *lifestyle* to Christian mission. That is a much, much harder calling. Why?

- Because it requires the adoption of an attitude that will unthinkingly shape your daily behavior.
- Because it requires a learning path that will intentionally unsettle your entire life and that of your family.
- Because it requires ingraining habits that will make you "odd" in the perceptions of your pagan neighbors.
- Because it requires taking risks with your career path and public image.

In the old days, you just had to be prepared to sacrifice your life if Viking "berserkers" broke into the church to rape and pillage. Today, you have to be prepared to change your lifestyle if Microsoft, Coca-Cola, or investment bankers break into your heart to rape and pillage.

Second, *how will you go about it*? In a world of micro-cultures and rapid change, the learning partners, content of information, and leverage points with which you prepare for ministry and learn from inevitable mistakes are very different from those of your former pastor and any Christian minister since about the sixteenth century. Why?

- Because just going to seminary won't prepare you for ministry anymore.
- Because deliberately *not* going to seminary won't prepare you for ministry either.
- Because today you learn more from music, movies, and relationships than you do from books, magazines, and lecturers.

• Because the world is changing so radically on a weekly basis that you don't know what you need to learn until you need to learn it.

In the old days, you had to be prepared to write a sermon, hold a meeting, or rush to the hospital in case somebody had a knotty theological problem, political crisis, or personal dilemma. Today, you have to be prepared to interject Jesus into a conversation, form a trusting relationship, and overcome control.

Third, *how will you be able to endure it?* This seems like an odd question, but in some ways it is the most important of all. If you devote your life to Christian ministry you will be pursuing a course of *least* credibility among the pagan publics of the world. You will have less respect than the garbage collector, and significantly less income. You will be required to have more knowledge than doctors, lawyers, and university professors, but receive much less recognition and have little prestige. You will place yourself and your family in harm's way.

Notice I have not raised the question *"What will it get you?"* This is the question most commonly asked of career counselors, but you are not asking it. This is because you already know that the only thing of which you can be sure is that Christian ministry will place you constantly alongside Jesus on his road to mission. That alone should suffice. If it does not, choose another path.

E-mail #5
Subject: Oddly Enough . . .

Dear Confused Christian:
I laughed when I read your post: "Oddly enough, Tom, my pastor also gave me three questions he thought I needed to answer. His questions were: a) Can the church use my particular gifts? b) Am I willing to acquire the right skills? c) Will I submit to denominational oversight? Your questions sound a bit different from his questions."

Of course they do. His questions are designed by the head office in Jerusalem that is looking for a few good people to run the programs in the Upper Room. My questions were designed by the disciples in the inn on the road to Emmaus, just after Jesus revealed himself in the breaking of the bread. His questions were developed by committee, voted by secret ballot, and engraved in the denominational polity. My questions were written on a napkin as the disciples were hastily pulling on their boots to follow Jesus down the road leading away from Jerusalem toward the general pagan public. You have to ask yourself which situation best describes the postmodern world.

The trouble with "education for church leadership" is that it begins with a misguided premise. It assumes the church should evaluate you for ministry. Today it's really the other way round. You evaluate the church for ministry. If the institutional church can help you follow Jesus on the road to mission, great! Connect with the church! If the church is going to sidetrack you from following Jesus on the road to mission, why bother to connect with the church?

The questions as your pastor has articulated them are ecclesiastically self-serving. They want to know if you have high gifts in mercy, administration, and communication. If so, they can more easily slot you in to be a good pastoral visitor, institutional manager, and preacher. They want to know if you are willing to learn the skills the institutional church considers important. If so, they can more easily slot you into a career path. They want to know if you will be loyal to the denomination. If so, they will guarantee you a pension and medical benefits.

Basically, there are two sets of key questions. There are two kinds of church expectations. There are two global contexts. The institutional church in the Christendom world will ask one set of questions. The missional movement in the pagan world will ask a different set of questions.

E-mail #6
Subject: Am I Unfair ... or Way Too Generous?

Dear Confused Christian:

I hear your protest. I do sound rather harsh. I have many good friends, deeply committed Christians, who are earnest about mission, and also faithfully working in regional and national judicatories and teaching in seminaries. I worked in national denominational office myself and have lectured in many seminaries. But the time for diplomacy is rapidly coming to an end.

This is no longer a world that needs church leaders. It is a world that needs mission movers. More and more denominational leaders and seminary teachers are also realizing this, and are incredibly frustrated with the ecclesiastical and modern education systems in which they function. The crisis is not just that churches are not recruiting clergy and that seminaries are not enrolling students. The crisis is also that denominations and seminaries are losing their best, brightest, most creative, and most mission-oriented leaders. They're fed up and leaving. They are fleeing to nonprofits, parachurches, independent consultancy, megachurches, international faculty appointments or whatever ... anything to get away from the dead-end ecclesiastical machines and theological factories that dominate North America. God bless them! And God help the institutions that they are leaving behind!

Is there time to change? Maybe. Is there a will to change? Maybe not. Some good people who remain associated with the head office in Jerusalem will say I am unfair. And some other good people who are way, way beyond Emmaus on the road to mission with Jesus will say that I am too generous.

All this, however, is beside the point. What about you? With ministry certification, training, and deployment all in chaos, where does that put you? How do you chart your course in the midst of this chaos? Let's take it one question at a time.

2

DO YOU REALLY WANT TO DO THIS?

E-mail #1
Subject: The Truth about Ministry

Dear Confused Christian:

"But Tom, when you ask, 'Do you really want to do this to yourself?' you make it sound like ministry is a pain and all my friends are right to say I'm nuts to even think about it."

About 50 percent of Christian ministry today is a pain in the backside. Ask any of the earliest church apostles, and they will tell you the same. After all, look what happened to them!

The apostles were accused of drunkenness, betrayed by the best givers, disappointed by smooth talkers, sabotaged by magicians, slandered by competitors, undermined by bureaucracy, held hostage by self-centered Corinthians, and continually sidetracked to the head office in Jerusalem. And that was from the Christians! Among the pagans they were shipwrecked, stoned, imprisoned, tortured, fined by the Internal Revenue Service, and thrown to the lions.

Now that Christendom is dead, most people who do go into the ministry do it for the wrong reasons, and soon burn out, drop out, or die out. They do it because they love the church, want to do good stuff, teach the right things, build a professional career, and get perspective on Christ. Now that used to be a pretty good life, because the church had cornered the niche market of spirituality. You could dabble in religion, do some beneficial service, and go home to a nice house. A person could shape the mission around a lifestyle and have a pretty good life. No more.

Today you have to *dare* to be a minister! You will only do it if you really, really desire to be with Jesus; want to multiply disciples who are in love with Jesus; urgently wish to bring welcome relief to people living self-destructive behavior patterns that they chronically deny; passionately model a spiritual life; and recklessly plumb the depths of Christ. You may or may not have a house, a pension plan, community respect, or many friends. Today you can't get away with shaping the mission around a lifestyle. You have to shape a lifestyle around a mission.

E-mail #2
Subject: Why Ministry Today Is a Pain

Dear Confused Christian:
"But that's what I want to do . . . *really* be with Jesus! Why would I experience that as a pain? I think it would be sheer pleasure!"

Part of the reason ministry is a pain is that the church has set you up with false expectations arising from the old "cold war" between the sacred and the secular of the twentieth century.

The established churches still think ministers should be called to defend the "sacred" world against the onslaughts of godless secularity. The world is their parish! Give them a trained professional, a standardized tactical toolbox, and enough money to buy ten acres of sacred land beside the expressway, and they will protect eternal truth from the raging sea of relativism until they die. Instead, you discover that your call is a "heartburst" for a particularly "wacko" micro-culture. They already believe in absolutes (they just don't know who

Jesus is), and all you really need to reach them is a living relationship with Christ, a big heart, and a kitchen table with at least three chairs.

The established churches make you think that your call will be a tidy career of therapeutic process and institutional permission that will lead you to mental health for yourself and corporate harmony for God's people. Instead, you discover that your call is a conspiracy of grace that is clear on purpose, vague on tactics, and scares the "bejeebers" out of the institution on which you will depend for your pension and medical benefits.

The other reason ministry is a pain is that, quite aside from scaring the institution that is supposed to pay your salary, you have to catch up with Jesus, who is already moving in a pagan world that fundamentally *does not like you.* You lead an outdoor worship service, and they'll pass a noise bylaw. You expand your parking lot, and they'll sue for environmental damage. You share Christ in Starbuck's, and they'll accuse you of bigotry. You innovate mission in the corporate or public sector, and they'll feed you to the lions or the IRS. I don't know if you are married or have a family, but being with Jesus in mission may not be what your husband signed up to do or your kids would welcome.

All I am saying is that you must clearly decide. Are you in it for mission, or philanthropy? For the gospel, or theology? For perfection or perks? For joy, or duty? For Christ, or Christianity? If you are in it for the latter reasons, ministry will be 50 percent pain in the backside and 50 percent modest career fulfillment. If you are in it for the former reasons, ministry will still be 50 percent pain—but the other 50 percent will be a joy and self-fulfillment that surpasses your wildest dreams.

E-mail #3
Subject: What Is a Call?

Dear Confused Christian:
I can understand why you are rethinking what a "call" is in the first place. A call only comes to people wildly desirous to be with

Jesus in mission. If you are not wildly desirous to be with Jesus in mission, what you are experiencing is not a call but a career move. You are evaluating all the job options that might fulfill your life, and are thinking that "ministry" might be more fulfilling than "medicine" or "teaching" or something else. But if you are wildly desirous to be with Jesus in mission, then you may experience a true "call." A call is an inexplicable desire to do something that is contrary to your natural inclination. It may be reckless. It may be distasteful. It may be dangerous. Yet you cannot rest until you attempt it. That's a call.

I keep making this contrast between the old world and the new, and I have to do so again.

In the old Christendom world, a "call" was a generic call to "the ministry" or "the world." It was a call to generalized tasks to preach the word, celebrate sacraments, care for the flock, and serve the community. The world would be your parish, and the institutional church would tell you where in that world you should be at any given time. You would then feel "called" to go there, open your toolkit to do the "word, sacrament, pastoral care, and service" *thing,* and grow the church.

In the emerging post-Christendom pagan world, a "call" is like that described in the Acts of the Apostles. A "call" and a "culture" go together. It is not a generic call, but a specific call to *this* micro-culture. It is not a call to perform certain special tasks, but a call to share the gospel with a zip code or affinity group. It's not about program, but about people. Paul had a vision of a Macedonian in Acts 16. You have a vision of a micro-culture in a chapter of your life. You do whatever it takes to reach that micro-culture. Later in life you will have another vision for another micro-culture— maybe in Ephesus or Cleveland, or Starbucks or the bowling alley—and you will go there. The "call" today is no longer a call to grow the church, but to grow disciples.

I have come to describe this as "heartburst." Your heart bursts for *this* particular people. Other people are good folks, but your heart bursts for this people, and so you devote your whole life to *this* people and no one else until you have another heartburst. So the question is: Who is *your* Macedonian? Who appears in your dreams at night saying, "Come over and help us?"

E-mail #4
Subject: What If There Is No Vision?

Dear Confused Christian:

"But Tom, what if I don't have a vision of a Macedonian? What if I really want to be with Jesus in mission, but I don't have particular people for whom my heart bursts yet?"

Then you must put yourself in the way of Christ. The Reformers might have said, "Wait upon the Lord," and the earliest church might have sent you away into the desert to meditate. If the world were a Christendom world and if the call were a generic call, then you could simply embark on a generic education for church leadership, acquire generic and transferable skills, and go about a generic one-size-fits-all ministry. But it isn't that kind of world and it isn't that kind of call. If you haven't identified the Macedonian, what challenges will you need to equip yourself to face? What companions will you need to accompany you? What language will you need to speak?

It all begins with a heartburst. If your heart does not burst for somebody, then there is no call in it to pursue. And hearts do not burst for institutions, or programs, or tasks. Hearts burst for people: flesh and blood, hurt and happy, culturally embedded people. The problem with traditional pastors educated for church leadership today is that they love the church but hate the people—or are at least indifferent to the people—who reside in their zip code.

E-mail #5
Subject: Who Exactly Is a "Heartburst"?

Dear Confused Christian:

Yes, I know I keep referring to "people" or groups within a zip code, but even that is a bit too general. You can understand "heartburst" best if you step back and reflect on how you sort out the diversity of the public.

The largest sorting is by "demographic": age, race, gender, income, family unit, relationship, housing, etc. One does not have a heartburst for a demographic. You may have a philanthropic concern for the poor, for example, but a "demographic" is simply too large and diverse for a heartburst.

The next largest sorting is by "lifestyle group": boomers, busters, upwardly mobile singles, empty-nesters, etc. Tex Sample, Arnold Mitchell, and research companies like Percept break out as many as 50-60 lifestyle groups in North America today, and you may have any number of them represented in your zip code, county census, or census tract. But one does not have a heartburst for a "lifestyle group" either. That is still too big and diverse. There are infinite variations of boomers and singles, for example, and some you will care about deeply and others not.

Finally, the smallest sorting is by "micro-culture": people who gather in this corner of the shopping mall food court, gather around these tribal symbols, are concerned about these issues, fighting these addictions, enthused by these opportunities . . . that sort of thing. Now those groups can be a "heartburst." I do not want to limit you, of course. A heartburst is simply an urgent desire to help a clearly defined group of people experience Jesus. They are "Macedonians" . . . and you desperately want to be among them, because that is where Jesus is.

A heartburst is a desire to connect *that* person with *this* hope. It is not a desire to include a micro-culture in the church program or membership, so much as a desire to help a micro-culture reshape purpose and life around Christ. You urgently want to give these particular people good reason to hope for the future. Can you give the people in this micro-culture a good reason to live another day and shape their lives around a higher purpose?

E-mail #6
Subject: Addressing Your Doubts

Dear Confused Christian:
It is normal for you to feel doubt about your calling. It is not normal for Christians to feel doubt about their baptism, but it is

normal for Christian leaders to feel doubt about their role in God's mission. Tragedy, pain, loss, and any form of gratuitous (unexplainable) evil can cause even the most confident Christians to question their Christian hope, and these may happen to you more than once in your life. The point, however, is that as a Christian minister your calling is not to identify with such moments in others, but to help others to overcome those moments in faith. If you can't do that, you cannot lead God's people into mission.

Of course this is hard! I know you are only human! God isn't asking you to stop being human. God is demanding that you start being a coach! Your role is not just to pretend to see, but to really see and articulate hope in the midst of hopelessness. You need to see spiritual gifts in the most sinful people, and spiritual possibilities in the most desperate situations, and spiritual potential in the most damning circumstances. No wonder, then, that you very commonly will doubt your ability—and in the experience of your own inevitable inadequacy, doubt your calling.

Once you have left the head office in Jerusalem, and are headed down the road to mission with Jesus, the definition of calling changes. A call is not the desire to accomplish that for which you are competent, but a desire to attempt that for which you are incompetent. A call is the surrender of your inevitable incompetency to Christ.

E-mail #7
Subject: Addressing Your Doubts about Your Doubts

Dear Confused Christian:
Here is a brief checklist that you can use to discern the authenticity of your calling. Use it whenever you question your calling throughout your life.

✓ *Am I in it for mission, or philanthropy?*
✓ *Am I in it for the gospel, or theology?*
✓ *Am I in it for joy, or duty?*

✓   Am I in it for perfection, or perks?
✓   Am I in it for Christ, or Christianity?

The truth is that the doubts you feel are less about God's calling, and more about your own self-worth. From the sixteenth
through the twentieth centuries, most Christian leaders believed
in their calling because it hurt so much. If it hurt, it must be have
been holy! They made sacrifices, compromised their holistic
health, and sometimes perished in the effort to prove their worth.
But in pre-modern and postmodern times, Christian leaders
believe in their calling because it feels so right. They do not need
to prove their worth because they are already confident in their
inherent value. They are not bad people hoping to make good,
but good people hoping to bless others. The verification of your
calling does not lie in low self-esteem and a need to be needed,
but in high self-esteem and a desire to share abundant life.

I realize that you have doubts about your calling. My question
is: Are these doubts emerging because you don't feel right about
the call, or because you don't feel right about yourself? You may
not deserve it, and it would not be surprising if you felt inadequate to do it, but *do you want it*? Is the call something that just
won't seem to let you go . . . and whenever it comes unbidden into
your mind, you can't help but smile?

E-mail #8
Subject: Doubts about Your Doubts about Your Doubts

Dear Confused Christian:
I see that you are still hung up over the issue of whether or not
you are worthy. You write: "I am just worried that I am not saintly,
intelligent, imaginative, or daring enough to do Christian ministry." It is your own "approach – avoidance" attitude that is your
biggest problem. You have to understand: *It's not about you in the
first place! It's about God's mission!* You approach the whole matter
of calling as if you personally were the focus of it. Look at the
Bible. God never chooses people who are particularly saintly,

intelligent, imaginative, or daring to do Christian ministry. In fact, the Bible tells you precious little about them. This is because they are unimportant. The mission is what is important. Your problem is that you want to "own" ministry as if it were a career choice. In fact, ministry "owns" you as a vehicle for its expression. I hate to break it to you—you are just a vessel, a clay pot to carry holy water.

Over the centuries of Christendom and modern living, people have gotten the false impression that it is the holiness of the individual that gives authenticity to the mission. In both ancient and contemporary times it is the other way around. It is the authenticity of the mission that gives holiness to the individual. The sacrament is not a sacrament because the priest is a priest, but the priest is a priest because the sacrament is a sacrament.

The fact that modernity has gotten it backwards is the reason why clergy today are both deified and vilified at the same time. On the one hand, modern Christians glorify the clergy, believing that their moral perfection and spiritual purity guarantees the efficacy of God's power. On the other hand, the inability of clergy to live up to impossible standards is easily blamed for the corruption of society and pervasiveness of sin. No wonder modernity can't recruit clergy! Who wants to be glorified and vilified all in the same day, seven days a week?

The more you persist in thinking that your calling is all about you, the more you set yourself up for this double deceit of clergy glorification and clergy vilification. You will never survive it, my friend! At the very beginning, you need to understand it never has been about you in the first place. It is simply about God's mission, and for better or worse you happen to be in the way of it. So if you have low self-esteem, you had better get over it if you want to be in Christian ministry. If God has chosen you, then God is giving you high self-esteem whether you like it or not. The last thing God's mission needs is somebody like you alternately strutting like a peacock and then lamenting "Poor me, poor me"!

I suppose that is why I have always liked John Wesley's covenant. It is reminiscent of the covenant of ancient pilgrims, medieval monks, and postmodern spiritual entrepreneurs. At the conclusion of his Watch Night liturgy, he writes:

> I am no longer my own, but thine. Put me to what thou wilt, rank me with whom thou wilt. Put me to doing, put me to suffering. Let me be employed by thee or laid aside for thee, exalted for thee or brought low for thee. Let me be full, let me be empty. Let me have all things, let me have nothing. I freely and heartily yield all things to thy pleasure and disposal.

If you can say those words without feeling a rush of self-esteem, then the problem is not that you do not like yourself very much but that you do not really like Jesus very much.

Unfortunately, covenants like these have been honored by intentional neglect. Modern churches have done everything possible to guarantee that clergy will be ranked with the best, never suffer, always have income, never be empty, have the closest parking spaces to the entrance . . . and also be responsible for every visit, blamed for every mistake, and crucified for every triviality. Avoid the heartache by getting this through your head: *It's not about you in the first place. It's about God's mission.*

E-mail #9
Subject: Am I in It for Mission, or Philanthropy?

Dear Confused Christian:

I really think that once you get beyond this issue of self-worth, you can use the five questions I shared earlier to settle your doubts once and for all. The first question to ask yourself is: *Am I in it for mission, or philanthropy?*

"Philanthropy" means "doing good stuff." There is absolutely nothing wrong with philanthropy. The world needs a lot more of it. In ancient Roman times, philanthropy was built into the very essence of social status. The expectation was that all public works and charities would be funded from the personal wealth of eminent citizens, and not from government subsidies. Our modern Christian notions of the "tithe" would have been considered quite a "comedown" by Marcus Aurelius and his friends, who believed citizens were expected to do far more than that for the public interest. Generally speaking, pagans make better philanthropists than Christians because "doing good stuff" is easier and more politically rewarding than "being a righteous person."

If your call is really to do "good stuff," then you are better off not being a Christian minister. Indeed, you are better off not being a Christian at all. If you just work it right, a good social activist can not only benefit the downtrodden, but also get elected to political office and increase her or his income. Republicans and Democrats do it all the time. Forgive me, I do not really mean to be snide. I am just pointing out that philanthropy has the double benefit of improving the lot of the underprivileged, while increasing the privileges of the philanthropist. That is why it is so attractive to the very best pagans.

In the twentieth century, a lot of men and women felt motivated to enter Christian ministry out of a desire to be "prophetic." As they staked out their identity, they rightly differentiated what it meant to be prophetic from the nineteenth-century cultural accommodation that thought "prophecy" was about mystical predictions of the future, but they wrongly failed to differentiate it from the twentieth-century cultural fascination with philanthropy. "Prophetic" leadership became a matter of "doing good stuff," "advocating good stuff," leading marches to do "good stuff," changing public policy to ensure "good stuff," or manipulating unimaginative or evil people to "do good stuff" whether they liked it or not. Two things resulted.

First, philanthropy bogged down in the latter decades of the century in endless debates about what "stuff" was really "good." Right- and left-wing political forces bashed heads, academics debated ideologies, and historical theology diffused into a myriad of "theologies of" this and that and every cultural perspective imaginable.

Second, Christian missions rapidly transformed into faith-based nonprofit agencies. Congregational life rapidly devolved into clubs that raised and managed charitable funds. Denominational unified budgets rapidly grew to dictate the mission agenda. And quarreling for control of denominational personnel and policy became the focus of energy for Christian leadership. Man, woman, youth, and child all saw themselves as "prophets," meaning that the philanthropic desire to "do good stuff" was at the center of their personal identity. Meanwhile, commitment and participation in the Christian movement among all the emerging micro-cultures took a dramatic "nose dive."

My point is that you think you might have a call into Christian ministry, and you had better figure out if it is a call to philanthropy or a call to mission. If it is a call to philanthropy, you will be very, very disappointed if you pursue that calling through the Christian movement. That movement is shrinking. There is less money, less political influence, less social prestige, and less corporate will within the established church with which to be philanthropic. As a philanthropic (or "prophetic") career path, it is bound to disappoint. That may be why many of the denominational "prophets" of the twentieth century are retiring early or changing career paths.

The difference between philanthropy and Christian mission is that the latter does not primarily seek to "do good stuff." It seeks to "multiply disciples of Jesus Christ." To be sure, the multiplication of disciples of Jesus Christ will likely result in lots of "good stuff" being done in the world, but the goal of Christian mission has more to do with "creating righteous people." This is really not a matter of "evangelism" (at least not as it has been characterized in modern times), because mission is not really a matter of conversion. Knowing and assenting to the right principles, or acknowledging and obeying prescribed behavior patterns, are not the same as living righteously and imitating Christ. Disciple multiplication is really a matter of changing attitudes, relationships, and life goals.

Do you feel called to multiply disciples of Jesus Christ? That is the question. Do you want to help people experience the transforming power of God (historically called "grace"), and then motivate and equip them to follow Jesus in their spontaneous and daring daily living (historically called "discipleship")? Exactly *how* you go about that is not my issue right now. My issue is whether or not you feel joyously compelled to do that, rather than merely doing "good stuff" to ease the oppression of various segments of the public. The latter will change demographics. The former will turn the world upside down. Do you want to increase the number of "righteous people" in the world by helping people trapped by self-destructive habits to experience the intervention of a higher power, identify this God as Jesus, and model their lifestyles after him?

If that is your passion, then you are indeed called to Christian ministry.

E-mail #10
Subject: Am I in It for the Gospel, or Theology?

Dear Confused Christian:

Thank you for sending me a few catalogues from some of the seminaries you are considering. In some of them I see articulated a program trend that has become quite common in the last decade. Their goal is to "train theologians." Speaking as a theologian (earned academic doctorate in philosophical theology and all), I urge you to avoid those seminaries if you are serious about your call to Christian ministry. No doubt both church and world need good theologians, and I am generally in favor of "theology" as a subject (along with philosophy, literature, and the liberal arts), but becoming a "theologian" will not equip you very well for Christian ministry. Many theologians who teach in academic institutions know this also, but in today's world of diminishing market share and greater competition, many Christian colleges and seminaries are finding it expedient to become centers for religious study rather than launching pads for Christian mission.

How do you experience and share the gospel? Do you experience and share it as "good news," or do you experience and share it as "welcome relief"? (You will recall the distinction in my book *Kicking Habits* by Abingdon Press.) Modern church people in the age of information have long treated the gospel as an intellectual commodity. It is a complex and profound collation of data, ranging from historical facts to personal perspective, that requires professional training to interpret and expound. The end result of this correctly interpreted and expounded "good news" is abstract dogma and ideological principle, which in turn can be debated endlessly in classrooms, coffee bars, and pulpit exchanges. This kind of "gospel" values rationality or verifiability, and encourages a kind of complacent passivity among people "in the know" that condescends to other people who "do not know enough."

Is this how you experience and share the gospel? Is your primary desire to verify the truth and share it in twenty-minute data bytes to adoring laity who respect your clergy credentials? Is your primary desire to teach a curriculum that will send everyone home with their curiosity about God satisfied, or to lead a protest that will finally entrench correct ethical principles in public policy? If so, your call is more about principle than people ... and more about theology than gospel.

On the other hand, you may experience and share the gospel as "welcome relief." This is how the gospel was experienced and shared in the earliest "mission to the gentiles," and it is how the gospel is experienced and needs to be shared by Christian ministers in the current pagan world. It is an experience of incarnation that is beyond rational explanation, that rescues people from their entrapment to sin and death (otherwise known as self-destructive behavior patterns that people chronically deny are robbing them of life). The gospel is not about verifiable data, but risky relationship. It is about grace, and the fruits of the Spirit that follow. This kind of gospel accepts the irrational, values the sacramental, and encourages a kind of restless compassion among "people on the way" to give away life to "people along the road." Theologians hope that people will exclaim, "I see! I understand! I get it now!" Christian missionaries hope that people will exclaim, "I am changed! I believe! God, that feels good!"

Is *this* how you experience and share the gospel? Is your primary desire to change lives, creating opportunities for grace through trusting and hopeful relationships? Is your desire to foment experiences that will motivate everyone into constant spiritual growth, or to equip spiritually gifted people to alter their lifestyles to be a blessing to every micro-culture outside the church? If so, then you really are called to Christian ministry.

E-mail #11
Subject: No, I'm Not against Thoughtfulness!

Dear Confused Christian:
I must say that I anticipated your complaint that I was painting a "black-and-white" picture. You are, after all, a very modern person. Even as a high school graduate you have already had more education than 98 percent of the world's population, and as a college graduate the assumption that education is the key to success and the vehicle of truth has been pretty well ingrained in your life. As a representative of the elite 2 percent of well-educated humanity, it is hard as a Christian to consider that the less-educated 98 percent are probably ahead of you in spiritual depth. You experience gratuitous evil, and have a psychological breakdown because you can't explain it. You experience unexplainable good, and have an intellectual crisis because you cannot control it. Meanwhile, the majority of Christians experience incredible evil, weep, pray, and keep on going. They experience astonishing grace, laugh, thank God, and keep on sharing. You stop, they keep going. Can you see anything wrong in this picture?

The mistake is in equating "education" with "thoughtfulness." The spiritual life demands thoughtfulness, but does not have to be educated. "Thoughtfulness" needs to be passionate, conversational, and disciplined, but it does not have to be certified, curricular, and scientific to be good thinking. The very best "educators" in any subject will always say that the worst thing about modern education is that it teaches people the thoughts of others without teaching people how to think for themselves. It breaks the universe of knowledge into tidy components without connecting the continuum of life into a meaningful whole—the kind of "thoughtfulness" that theologians and ideologues rarely consider.

Amid all the competing Christian "theologies" available in the world, there are but two approaches to the spiritual life. There is the "modern" approach and the "pre- or postmodern" approach.

The "modern" approach assumes that people start their spiritual journey by doing "reflection," and that this will lead to such perceptive understanding that they will feel "compassion," and that this loving sentiment will in turn result in "action." Action will raise questions that an individual has never asked before, and send them back into "reflection." This unending circle of *reflection-compassion-action* has been the dominant spiritual method of Christianity since Constantine institutionalized the church. It accelerated after the invention of the printing press, was embedded in European Protestantism, and became refined through the Age of Enlightenment to be uncritically assumed by North American Christendom.

- *If only people would really read and study the Bible, they would understand the true nature of sin. They would have compassion on themselves and others, and take action to convert the world. In the course of that crusade, they will undoubtedly ask new questions and return to the Bible for answers.*
- *If only people would raise their consciousness and study demographic realities about race, gender, and the economy, they would understand the true nature of oppression. They would have compassion on themselves and others, and take action to reform society. In the course of that crusade, they will undoubtedly ask new questions and seek experts for the answers.*

This is why literacy guilds are so aggressive and higher education so popular. It is not simply that education will bring career success. It is the deeper, hidden assumption that education is the door to the spiritual life.

It is this perception of the spiritual life that fires seminaries to "train theologians" and denominations to "train professionals." They really do believe in the spiritual life, and that the door into it is thoughtful reflection. Unfortunately, it rarely works that way in a pagan world.

The second approach to the spiritual life worked best in the pre-modern, largely illiterate, pagan world of the past ... and works best today in the postmodern, image-based, pagan world of the present. This is the world of story, mentoring relationship, irrational experience, and risk-taking entrepreneurship. This approach assumes that people start the spiritual life with non-rational, passionate experiences of the Holy. These experiences may be joyous and/or fearful, and they alter both identity and lifestyle. That these alterations are for *the good* may in fact only be revealed at a later time. This experience of radical humility drives people to thoughtful reflection in order to sort out the meaning and implication of that confusion of *agape* and *eros* that has changed their lives. The compassion that follows completes the process of being swept away by the Holy, as people focus love beyond themselves. In the course of compassion, they meet the incognito Christ among the public again and encounter the Holy.

This unending cycle of *experience-thoughtfulness-compassion* is the alternate expression of the spiritual life that has lingered at the margins of Christendom and is now once again coming into its own.

Which cycle is a truer description of your spiritual life? Forgive me the history lesson. Let's make this personal. If you want to assess the authenticity of your calling in Christian ministry, then you must see that calling as emerging from your true spiritual life and not just as a vocational choice.

I know you. We have had a long association. Although you are "modern" enough to be swayed by the bias to higher education, in fact your spiritual life has never depended on it. You drifted through three careers, two marriages, five philosophies of life, six states of consciousness, and umpteen self-destructive habits until you were seized by a Higher Power who scared the heck out of you. You thought about the meaning and implications of that experience long and hard with mentors and peer groups, through intimate relationships and trial-and-error experimentation. The more you surrendered to God, the more you thought about your destiny; and the more you thought about the fulfillment of life, the more you recognized that fulfillment in loving people beyond yourself and even more than yourself.

Ultimately, your compassionate immersion into the life and well-being of others led you to encounter God all over again in an unpredictable collage of face, color, and personality. Whether it hurt you or helped you, it swept you off balance and precipitated humility that at times felt more like humiliation. There was no "reflection" here, no intellectual pondering. Instead you felt that original sense of awe all over again. The experience of the Holy might be hot or cold—devouring fire or refreshing breeze—but it left you speechless, helpless, and what is more, thoughtless. Ideas just ran out, like a paved road vanishing into the primordial jungle. Then the brooding thoughtfulness began to kick in, and the compassion, and the cycle repeated itself.

In other words, the core of your spiritual life has been the gospel, not theology. Certainly, you valued expert advice and professional coaching to help you live that spiritual life. My point is that it did not *replace* that spiritual life. Don't let your bias for modernity divert you from the spiritual life that you have.

E-mail #12
Subject: Am I in It for Joy, or Duty?

Dear Confused Christian:
I see I caught your attention by helping you see your calling as an extension of your spiritual life. You can see the importance of this by observing the latest trends in clergy burnout and disability. I think one of the reasons you doubt your calling is that you observe all too many professional clergypersons on the brink of exhaustion because fundamentally they have no "life." Their personal life, relational life, emotional life, physical life, and even intellectual life have all been sacrificed for the sake of their

careers. No, that is unfair. For many devoted clergy it is not that shallow ... and the self-destructive behavior is more profound. They have sacrificed "life" for the sake of an obsessive, burdensome sense of obligation to God, to church, to ecclesiastical polity, or to heritage. This disconnection between "having a life" and "pursuing a calling" is what lies at the end of the trail for modern spirituality that starts with education first, and then grinds inexorably toward professionalism, privilege, and hierarchical authority. It is really *this* that you fear, is it not?

But this does not have to happen if you ground your calling in a spiritual life that starts from the very beginning with holistic experience, and only then moves on to thoughtful reflection. You can "have a life" and "pursue a calling" at the same time. The one does not compete with the other, but each leads seamlessly into the other.

This is why the question you want to ask is "Am I in it for joy, or duty?" Those who are motivated to pursue Christian ministry from a sense of duty are paying God back for favors received. They see it not just as self-sacrifice, but as sacrifice of *self*. This kind of spiritual life sounds noble, but it predisposes you to enact leadership patterns that ultimately drive you to drink, divorce, and depression. In fact, the spiritual life that should give expression to Christian ministry is a quest for self-fulfillment. It leads to leadership patterns that are not only healthier for you, but also more effective for God's realm. Here is the contrast:

The obligation of career	The life of fulfillment
Leader and follower	Coach and team
Parent and family member	Pilgrim among pilgrims
Manager to volunteers	Motivator to missionaries
Servant to masters	Entrepreneur to partners

What you really fear is that if you pursue Christian ministry, you will follow a career of unending obligation. It starts nobly enough, and it is a wonder to witness the egocentricity of most ordination ceremonies. How they exalt the clergy! Clergy become the programmatic leaders who will impose on the community core values, beliefs, vision, and mission. They are the parents of Christians who grow up beyond adolescence, and they hold their hands through all the stages of life until they die. But just watch these ordained clergy as the years of professional service take their toll. They lose purpose and meaning scrambling to recruit volunteers to implement an institutional agenda. Ultimately, they cease being servants of the Master, and become slaves to a multitude of "masters" ranging from Aunt Nellie, who requires a visit from the pastor because she suffers with a bunion, to the bishop who requires attendance by the pastor for the latest politically correct indoctrination retreat.

Be of good cheer! It does not have to be that way for you. If you start out fulfilling the spiritual life as you have known it, you can be a coach among teammates for Christ—a spiritual traveler who does not have to have all the answers, nor take care of fellow passengers, but who shares and receives spiritual insights and practical support. You can motivate people to fulfill their own destinies and pursue their own mission without having to do it for them. You can be as creative and cutting-edge as you wish, confident that the Christians around you are not critics evaluating your every move and sermon, but partners who can be expected to behave kindly and think independently. Every Christian is bid to lead a spiritual life. Let them do it! Insist that they do it! Your calling is not to do it for them, but to model it and coach it.

Of course, if you walk down this alternative path, you can probably expect friction with your institutional superiors and denominational colleagues. If you choose to be ordained, do not expect me to bow down in awe, burn incense, chant ecstatically, or treat you any differently. Surrender the ego at the outset, and it will be easier to accept yourself later on.

I was once with a gathering of clergy (from various denominations) and asked the rather innocuous question "Do you enjoy ministry?" I couldn't believe the reaction. Most of them looked bewildered, having no idea how to answer the question. It just did not compute in the context of their weekly agendas. Some of them got very angry. How *dare* I even think that ministry should be something that is "enjoyed"! Ministry, they said, was a high calling, a sacred trust, a solemn responsibility, etc., etc. Most of their spouses and children (if they were still living together) would have simply said it was an intolerable burden that rendered otherwise kind and intelligent people insufferable bores.

The question is not just legitimate, but crucial. Will you *enjoy* ministry or not?

The manner in which church leaders answer this question for themselves parallels the manner in which church participants answer such a question. Most churches practice some form of spiritual gifts discernment among their congregational members. What churches *do* with that information, however, represents the difference between duty and joy. Some churches proceed to match the individual gifts of participants with their own list of institutional or programmatic needs. People are "slotted in" wherever there is a nominations vacancy or a program vacuum. They assume people will be content simply in the exercise of their gift—even if it is for somebody else's mission! Other churches proceed to counsel the individual participants to go the next step and discern how they can use their gift to be a blessing to others and so fulfill their own personal mission. They assume that people will only be fulfilled if somebody equips and networks them to pursue their *own* gifted and called ministry with excellence.

Although both churches call this "lay empowerment," you can guess the result. The former church leaves behind a trail of burned-out laity who have done their duty and feel sadly empty inside. The latter church multiples motivated laity who are fulfilling themselves and having a whale of a good time. The former church has a five-year strategic plan and no volunteers to implement it. The latter church has no idea what the mission agenda will be next year, but an enormous volunteer pool charging off in all directions.

Something similar is happening with the deployment of clergy. You see it as you ponder your own calling to Christian ministry and it worries you. Most denominations help candidates discern their call and hone their skills, and then deploy them to serve mission agendas that are not really their own. Whether or not the denomination uses an "appointment" process or a "call" process is irrelevant, because the ultimate goal is the same. Match the professional skill with the institutional need. This scares you, and you feel so guilty about being scared that you doubt your calling. How can something like surrender to an ecclesiastical mission agenda sound so right, and feel so wrong?

You need to go with your intuition. This kind of mission agenda is wrong. It is just as wrong as insisting that laity must match their gifts to institutional needs. The only really faithful thing to do is to discern your gifts, hear your call, and fulfill your vision. By all means do it in as large a companionship of fellow pilgrims as possible, but whether that companionship is large or small, traditional or atypical, fulfill your destiny. Shape the job around the destiny . . . don't warp the destiny to accommodate the job! That is what it means to "enjoy" the ministry.

E-mail #13
Subject: Am I in It for Perfection, or Perks?

Dear Confused Christian:

I really don't blame you for asking about salary guidelines, pension and medical benefits, and vacation expectations as you consider whether or not you will devote yourself to Christian ministry. After all, if you really do aim to "live a life" and not just "do your duty," these practical matters are important. There is nothing particularly holy about being unable to afford medical treatment or university education for your children, and there is nothing particularly saintly about living in housing or eating food that is inferior to the standard of the community in which you live. And I, for one, would never want to have to retire to some low-budget seniors' center reserved for impoverished and discarded clergy.

No, I don't blame you for wanting some reassurances about security for the future of yourself and your family. What is reprehensible is using those securities as tools for contentment rather than resources for continuous personal and spiritual growth. The reasonable and faithful quest for holistic health and the "enjoyment" of ministry models the spiritual life for others. What kind of model would it be if you accepted abuse and needlessly placed your family at risk, not because you pursued a dangerous vision, but because you kept company with uncaring institutional church members who refused to pay you enough? On the other extreme, what kind of model would it be if you accepted the use of free automobiles, golf course memberships, and the best seats in restaurants simply because you kept company with elite institutional church members hoping to buy your personal attention? Both the self-flagellating prophet and the high-living evangelist may use security as perks, whether in denial or acquisition, to enhance their personal power.

For better or worse in today's North America, those who devote themselves to Christian ministry will probably never rise above a middle-middle class economic status. They will place themselves in greater jeopardy of reducing their income and financial security than raising it. In part this is because Christian faith communities are generally losing wealth, as they become minorities in a larger pagan culture. In part this is because pagan culture is slowly eroding the nontaxable benefits that a Christendom world offered the clergy. Mostly, however, this is because Christian leaders must now work as entrepreneurs rather than as employees. In the modern world, a larger salary seniority scale in the denomination or congregation guaranteed their incomes. In the postmodern world, those same denominations or congregations either do not have the money, or faithful Christian ministers are realizing that accepting money on their terms compromises the pursuit of a Christian vision.

What you really need to think about is not whether you will have enough income to survive and sufficient perks to thrive, but rather whether your sources of income will sustain holistic growth and whether your additional perks will compromise your calling. In ancient terminology, you are called to perfection, not professionalism. Not that you have now, or will ever attain that perfection this side of heaven! The point is that you both model and coach the pursuit of that perfection for others. The pagan public is not stupid. They can smell hypocrisy a mile away. Unnecessarily harmful poverty and unnecessarily beneficial wealth undermine the credibility of any spiritual leader.

Some people are attracted to Christian ministry for the perks. They do not last long, because they grow bitter watching their income stagnate while church members squander money on property maintenance and Florida vacations. Ironically, other people are attracted to Christian ministry for the lack of perks. They do not last long either, because they cannot bring themselves to value the generosity God's spirit elicits from disciples. Neither is faithful. Only those who are in it for perfection will last very long and be trusted by the public.

E-mail #14
Subject: Dual Career?

Dear Confused Christian:

I think you missed the point of my earlier message. You write: "Don't worry about my obsessing over perks! My spouse has a good full-time job, so I am less worried about income from the church." I gather you consider that situation to be a blessing. I would consider that situation to be such a burden that it might well undermine your credibility and compromise your calling altogether. What is it you want to model for the public—that Christian calling is a hobby permitted to those who are otherwise financially independent? And why would you release a congregation from their full responsibility to care financially for the full health and well-being of their pastor and the pastor's family? If you devote yourself to Christian ministry because you can afford to do it, you are tacitly declaring that perks come before perfection. Better that you should devote yourself to ministry even though you *cannot* afford to do it.

In recent years, there has been a huge growth in second-career, dual-income clergy. Too many of these people are secretly prioritizing perks over perfection, and it is undermining the credibility of clergy in general and harming the Christian mission to the pagan public. They give the *appearance* of poverty, and live a *real-*

ity of wealth, and that is more harmful than either poverty or wealth by itself. They come to church in an older model car, but that is only because it is the second car in the family. They dress modestly "at work," and dress elaborately "at leisure." They preach boldly about self-sacrifice, when in actual fact they sacrifice very little. They advocate dangerous and controversial public policies, but return from the fray to comfortable living rooms and excellent wine. But the worst crime of all is that they allow Christian congregations to compromise their own quest for perfection by removing money from the cost of discipleship. Indirectly, these unfaithful clergy entice other Christian folk into their folly.

Sure, sure, I understand that you are "only trying to help poor urban or rural churches who otherwise couldn't financially survive." Let them die, then. God does not beckon them to financially survive, but to quest for perfection. Better that they close the doors of the building and bury the institution than that they allow the likes of you to lead them astray. Even the devil can be generous, if by so doing it will take people away from an authentically spiritual life. Let them sell the property and meet as a cell group in the apartment buildings and restaurants and living rooms of the community, if that is what it takes to afford the leadership that they need.

I begin to fear that I have misjudged your intentions. I begin to think that the real reason you are considering devoting your life to Christian ministry has nothing to do with "helping poor urban and rural churches survive," and everything to do with finding a beneficial service project that will ease your affluent, guilty conscience. I do too much e-mail with real Christian inquirers to waste time on this.

E-mail #15
Subject: Living with Ambiguity

Dear Confused Christian:
I am greatly relieved to receive your latest message! I have prayed that either I was mistaken, or that you would awaken, or both. I think both have happened.

I understand now that what you are really wrestling with is the ambiguity that increasingly burdens every paid Christian leader today. You write: "Isn't the bottom line that the very phrase *salaried minister* is a contradiction in terms?" Yes, I think you are right. Every human being is spiritually gifted, and every Christian is called to ministry. So why should a few get paid for it? The ambiguity is not really resolved by saying that "Christian ministers are *leaders*" because in the postmodern Christian movement in the pagan world, adult spiritual growth and leadership development are the same thing. Every Christian must be a "leader" of the mission that God has elicited from his or her heart. Nor is the ambiguity resolved by saying that "Christian ministers are *skilled* leaders" because in a fast-changing world everyone is incompetent at any given instant. Everyone must constantly *acquire* and *reacquire* skills on a daily basis, so why should a few get paid for it?

The Christendom tradition is that certain people are "set apart" or "called out of the body of Christ" in order to do four things: celebrate the sacraments, teach the word, care for God's people, and serve in Christ's name. As strategic plans go, this made better sense in the Christendom world of the past 1500 years or so than it does in the post-Christendom world of today.

Depending on one's theology, a good case can be made to set aside specific people to celebrate the sacraments. If you understand the sacraments (whether two or seven or more) to be holy experiences made possible only through the mediation of a priest, then ordination makes sense. I am not arguing whether this belief is right or wrong, or even how this belief might be right or wrong, only that if you believe this it makes sense to isolate a few Christians from the rest of the Christian community for an exclusive ministry. Ordination without some exalted view of sacrament makes little sense otherwise. What does remain ambiguous, however, is *why these people should be paid*. Why should ordination, in and of itself, require a salary, pension, and medical benefits?

The other three reasons to "set apart" specific Christians from the body of Christ has morphed considerably in the transition to the postmodern world. All Christians are supposed to communicate the word well and rightly, and all Christians are supposed to care for each other, and all Christians are supposed to serve in the name of Christ. If "skill" is no longer a viable indicator, in what sense should a few be different from the rest? To persist in pressing an outdated notion on the new world of instant change only serves to give a few people an exaggerated opinion of their worth, and lets the rest of the people off the hook in regard to spiritual growth. And that is precisely what is happening.

On the other hand, the same fast-paced world that no longer needs people with standardized skills to do the ministries for us increasingly needs people with contextual abilities to help us to do it for ourselves. Their function is that of "tutor," "trainer," and "coach" instead of teacher, caregiver, and servant. These do seem to be special people, and one wonders how to train them and whether or not they can be "certified" in any credible way. But that, too, is an issue to debate another time.

The real question you have identified is this: Should even these tutors, trainers, and coaches *be paid*? Should they receive non-taxable benefits like homes and housing allowances, or book and continuing education allowances, or travel allowances? Should they receive a salary, a stipend, or an allowance? How big is too big and how small is too small? If there is one, should it vary by seniority, or academic training, or popularity, or community context?

I don't think anyone has the definitive answer to these questions. These are tactics, and in the present time of radical and unpredictable change, all tactics are up in the air. My guess is that during the next twenty years or so of transition into the post-modern, post-Christendom world, this ambiguity will be both inescapable and uncomfortable. A few things are becoming clear:

- Whether you receive a salary and wonder if you shouldn't, or whether you don't receive a salary and wonder if you should, you really do need to constantly wrestle with the issue. It is not a "given" anymore.
- Most Christian ministries are evolving toward volunteer, unpaid positions or teams. Better to have a large con-

tinuing education budget for volunteers than a lot of paid and pensioned office holders.

• Decisions about who is paid or unpaid are increasingly made "bottom up" rather than "top down." They are made from within any given context for the context, and not imposed from a hierarchy.

• Contextual income decisions have more and more to do with "credibility," and less and less to do with "expertise." That means "certification" no longer translates into "salary increase."

In the midst of this financial uncertainty, the question I asked you earlier returns with even more force. Are you in it for perks or perfection? If you are in it for financial security and benefits, the long-term prospects are worrisome. Most people will choose other paths. On the other hand, if you are in it to pursue, model, and coach "perfection," all the risks will be worth it.

E-mail #16
Subject: Am I in It for Christ, or Christianity?

Dear Confused Christian:

Apparently my approval or endorsement of your intentions to become ordained is important to you, for you have even given up hinting and are now asking directly if I think you are truly called. This need you have for the approval of an authority figure betrays an ambiguity in your own heart that must be resolved before you risk all to follow Jesus on the road to mission.

I remember when we first met. It was during one of those "vocational awareness" events sponsored jointly by the denomination and the seminary for college students wondering about their future. I forget whether you were a religion or a sociology major, but I do recall you scored high on spiritual gifts for "mercy," "counseling," "helping," and "administration." Each speaker at the event hammered home messages like: The Church Needs Leaders, and Remember How Much the Church Has Given to You and the World, and God Sets Apart Leaders from the Laity, and You Love the Church, Don't You? I watched your eyes light up and your ego puff up, and when you zealously declared that you believed you were "called," I thought to myself that you were one of the most sincere and utterly naïve Christians I had ever met. I also thought that you are pretty typical of the kind of "lion fodder" that usually attends seminary, serves five years in the parish, and then burns out, drops out, or opts out for another career.

Now, you have come a long way since then, as even this e-mail conversation reveals, and for what it is worth I have a higher regard for your sense of call than I did then. Of course, my opinion isn't really worth much, as I shall explain. I say this not out of self-deprecation (as you know I am anything but modest), but because when it comes to "discerning an authentic call" nobody's opinion (especially that of judicatories, seminaries, or other authorities) is worth very much.

And this brings me to the last question: *Are you in it for the sake of Christ, or for the sake of Christianity?*

This is an old, old question that has been asked repeatedly by monastics, reformers, prophets, visionaries, crotchety old men, and bold young women, but the fact that it is a question that has to be repeated so often reveals that the choice is more difficult than most people imagine. When you first answered the question some years ago, you scoffed at the choice as a "no-brainer" and said that *of course* your call was to Christ rather than to the institutional expressions of Christ. Yet here you are, years later, still looking for the approval of some authority to endorse your discernment of call! Oops! The question isn't so easy to answer, is it?

E-mail #17
Subject: Am I *Really* in It for Christ After All?

Dear Confused Christian:
The amazing thing about addiction is that addicts not only deny they have a problem, but they quite sincerely and intelli-

gently deflect criticism toward some sidetrack of rationalization that can be endlessly debated. This carries away the conversation so that the real issue of addiction is ignored in the heat of an essentially trivial debate. You demonstrated that addictive behavior pattern very well in your last letter to me. In that letter you reiterated your commitment to Christ, and then launched into a diatribe against the institutionalization of the church that has accommodated itself to all the materialism and paraphernalia of culture.

However, we are not talking about a choice between "Christ" and "culture," and I will not accept your subtle imposition of co-dependency to sidetrack us from the real issue of addiction. We all know that the relationship between "Christ" and "culture" is both necessary and ambiguous, and we can profitably spend lots of time sorting it out *after* you have come to grips with your abiding addiction to "Christianity." Culture will be involved in your mission no matter what, so get over it. The degree of integrity with which you handle the ambiguities of Christ and culture, however, will largely be determined by your *unambiguous* choice between Christ and Christianity.

Just as Jesus was tempted by the devil at the beginning of his ministry, so also you are being tempted by the devil before and during your ministry. This is a temptation that will never go away. It is built into the ambiguity of the incarnation itself. Once the pre-existent Word became flesh, the potential for finitude to be raised to the status of ultimate concern became even more tempting than ever before. In the same way, once the experience of Christ becomes "enfleshed" by Christianity, the temptation to elevate Christianity to the status of ultimate concern becomes even more tempting to Christian leaders than ever before.

Christ is to Christianity as the meaning of a sentence is to the syntax of a sentence, or as the import of a symbol is to the symbol itself. The meaning requires an articulation, but as soon as it is articulated not only is the meaning limited, the articulation usurps the centrality of the meaning. The import demands a symbol through which it can be revealed, but if the symbol stops pointing to the import that lays beyond it the symbol itself becomes demonic. By "demonic," I mean that the finite form claims an ultimacy that it does not truly possess. It demands an allegiance of the heart that it does not deserve. It influences human behavior in a manner that betrays human nature. The ever-present temptation of Christianity is that the mysterious depth of God may be replaced by various expressions of God.

It is not hard to find examples of Christian leaders succumbing to this temptation. Remember, the issue here is not materialism or wealth per se. It is entirely possible for meaning to be articulated through uneducated speech or grand rhetorical preaching, and it is possible for divine import to be revealed through tinplate or solid gold, and either poverty or wealth can entrap the unwary Christian leader. There is an arrogance to poverty as well as an arrogance to wealth.

Music, architecture, polity, and office are the most common sources of temptation. Those who are in it for Christianity end up staking everything in the defense of so-called "sacred" music and architecture, or "appropriate" polity and "correct" offices. Of course, the music might be classical or easy listening, and the architecture might be cathedral or industrial; the polity might be this denomination or that denomination, and the offices might be that of the clergy or the caretaker. Yet church wars will be fought over them all precisely because naïve church leaders have surrendered to the temptation to worship the forms of spirituality in neglect of the depth of God.

Do you see that the choice between Christ and Christianity depends on a fundamental attitude of your spirit?

E-mail #18
Subject: The "Protestant Principle"

Dear Confused Christian:
Well, I see that you do not yet see the real temptation of "Christianity" that tests your professed commitment to Christ. You write: "But Tom . . . isn't it true that some cultural forms are

better than others in communicating Christ? Isn't the media really the message?"

You seem to be confusing Marshall McLuhan with Augustine. If it were true that some cultural forms (some music, some architecture, some polity, some offices) were "better" than others in communicating God, then grace would mean nothing and higher education would mean everything. Indeed, that is what the devil and modernity would have you think. It is what they have convinced the church to believe as true for several centuries. Hence, the stress on Sunday school, catechism, and liturgical reform. "If only people could appreciate organ music, historic buildings, ecclesiastical hierarchy, and the authority of seminary graduates, they would experience God more perfectly." Rubbish! That's Christianity talking! What Christ says is that he can turn water into wine whenever he chooses. He can heal whomever he wishes, and organize in any way that works, and use former tax collectors and illiterate fisherman to hand out God's food and drink.

When I used the word "addiction" to refer to Christianity in my former post, I meant that literally. Christianity is like a prescription drug. Prescribed and taken in proper doses, and with a "grain of salt," it enhances the health of the Christian pilgrim. Obsessively abuse it to maintain a sentimental high, and it will kill you. Christianity acts like a drug on the faithful Christian. Gradually it supplants true spiritual health in the depth of Christ with a façade or imitation of health that is a mere sentiment, or a mere dogma, or a mere institution. Yet the drug users are so beside themselves that they go on defending, protecting, and romanticizing their drug supply until their church is dead. Alas, too many denominational leaders and clergy supply the drugs, and too many board members and veteran church members overdose on them. Have you ever read about the opium dens, and the vacant, staring residents living amid the smoke? Have you ever visited a church, and seen the "dead eyes" of the worshipers mouthing hymns amid the incense? Same thing.

Say "No!" to drugs. That is what one great theologian described as "The Protestant Principle" (Paul Tillich, *The Protestant Era*). It is the fundamental bottom-line refusal to make Christianity of higher concern than Christ. It is the response of Jesus to the temptations of the devil: *Away with you, Satan! For it is written, "Worship the Lord your God, and serve only him."* The principle of negation is not only "Protestant" of course. The early monks said "No!" against the church establishment, just as evangelicals, charismatics, social justice advocates, and mavericks of all ages have said it against the snobbery of whatever in-group of liturgically correct, dogmatically pure factions happened to be dominant at the time. Christ uses *and shatters* Christianity. And the question is: Are you going to be allied with the apocalyptic power of Christ, or with the denominational pension plan?

E-mail #19
Subject: The Demonic Power of "Approval"

Dear Confused Christian:
"Can't it be both?" It seems to me we wrestled with this desire to "have our cake and eat it too" before. No, I am not trying to pit "Christ" and "denomination" against each other! I am saying that the *experience of Christ* and the *expressions of Christ* necessarily go together precisely because the *salvation of Christ* is intended to be *shared with others*. If the experience of Christ were only a personally enlivening mystical experience, then it would not have to be expressed (articulated, communicated, celebrated, shared). But that would be Gnosticism, not Christianity. As long as the great commandment *compels* us to share the experience of Christ, then infinite meaning must somehow be conveyed through finite forms.

But this dynamic relationship between experience and expression is not the whole story. If there is a compulsion to share the experience, so also there is a compulsion to resist the experience. We see this time and time again ... and you will suffer this reality frequently if you truly respond to your call. The more passionate, eloquent, and urgent a leader is to express Christ to others, the more resistant, intransigent, and hostile some church participants will become to the experience of Christ for them-selves. I am not talking about the general pagan public, mind you. I am talking about the intransigence of the *church, of Christianity*. Usually this intransigence is not revealed through outright con-flict (although there is enough of that), but through dogged obe-dience to specific forms of Christian expression. *This* liturgy, *this* musical genre, *this* translation of Scripture, *this* organizational method, *this* church architecture are imposed as normative for Christian behavior. These "forms" are elevated to have ultimate concern, and so deflect the urgency to experience the formless depths of Christ.

I know that you have heard the talk about "spiritual warfare," but much of that literature is still a shallow misrepresentation of the *real* war being fought for the hearts of Christian believers. Believe me, the devil has little need to corrupt culture, if instead he can sidetrack the hearts of Christian believers to the trivial pur-suit of preserving so-called "sacred" expressions of the Holy! While Christianity sits in debate about what is sacred or secular, the road to mission grows weeds.

Yet this "Christianity" is exactly who you want approval from in order to be a Christian leader! The need for approval, and the arro-gance of the church in believing it can give or withhold permission to be a Christian leader, is part of the demonic power that resists the experience of Christ. By all means, get perspective, gather opinions, pray for discernment with your most-trusted spiritual guides, con-nect with the greatest mentors, seek after the best training, work in the most mutually supportive team … do all of this … *but do not found your decision to follow Christ into ministry on the approval of any ecclesiastical authority!* If the prophets had done so, none of them would have prophesied. If John the Baptist had relied on the permis-sion of the scribes, he would never have baptized anyone (although he probably would have kept his head and retired with a pension plan). If Peter and John had waited for Gamaliel to certify them, the Christian movement would have stayed in Jerusalem and perished.

If it is God's grace that calls you, then you do not need permis-sion. And if you are so in need of permission, then it is almost cer-tainly not God's grace that calls you.

At the very beginning, with the first inkling or first suspicion that God might be calling you to ministry, you face the choice. Will it be Christ or Christianity? Choose Christ, and your denomination can still help you grow and perfect yourself as a mission leader. Choose Christianity, and having tied the calling itself to the approval of an institution, you will be entrapped by an obligation to preserve the expressions of Christ rather than live in the depths of Christ.

E-mail #20
Subject: You Really Do Want to Do This!

Dear Christian Companion:

I wept when I received your last post. Such a simple, touching, surrender of yourself to the grace of God! I thank God that you are called. You are in it for mission, not philanthropy. You are in it for the gospel, not theology. You are in it to fulfill your destiny in joy, not obligation to an institution. You are in it questing for perfection in a spiritual life, not seeking perks and privileges in a career path. You are in it for Christ—to experience the depths of Christ, and to invite others to plunge into those depths wearing whatever "diving gear" they find most useful.

My tears, however, are really elicited because of your courage. You have overcome your old naiveté about Christian leadership, not merely with knowledge, but with audacity. Your courage is more important than your skill in the "circus maximus" of this pagan world. When the lions are loose, and the crowd jeers, it may be just you and Christ. No "megachurch." No "successful career." No "ecumenical applause." Just you and Christ in the arena ... and that will be more than sufficient.

3

HOW WILL YOU GO ABOUT IT?

The Right Partnerships

E-mail #1
Subject: Celebration and Caution

Dear Christian Companion:

I can sense your excitement and feel your urgency now that you have really clarified your calling. You write: "I am definitely 'in it' because I want to be with Jesus in mission. I want to share the gospel as welcome relief. And I really want to multiply disciples and model a spiritual life that plumbs the depths of Christ! I see precisely the people for whom my heart breaks, and I am desperate to be among them with the gospel! Wow!" That "Wow!" is the passion that reveals the authenticity of your call. Unfortunately, if you are not careful, the next three years of seminary followed by your first five years of indentured service to the denomination are very likely going to beat the "Wow!" right out of you.

E-mail #2
Subject: Why the Wow Wavers

Dear Christian Companion:

"Dear Tom: What is it with you? What *is* your problem with seminary?"

My fundamental problem with seminary is that it is a center of higher education. Ironically, that is the one thing I valued most of all leaving university in the modern world, and it is the one thing that has been most debilitating entering ministry in the postmodern world. I really don't want that to happen to you.

What I mean to say is that seminary is *merely* a center of higher education, and therefore the "Wow!" has very little place in it. Oh yes, there is plenty of room for "Aha!" in a center of higher education. One can penetrate to remarkable insight. Yet there is a remarkable resistance to be penetrated by remarkable insight. The "Wow!" is treated with suspicion, subjected to critical judgment, de-mythologized, rationalized, psychoanalyzed, and generally rendered either innocuous or (surprise, surprise!) supportive of the seminary's liberal or conservative ideological agenda. Seminaries are centers of higher education, and the best they can do is approach the prophetic. They will never touch the apocalyptic. And since the pre- and postmodern worlds are open to the apocalyptic they are inadequate at best.

You see, the "Wow!" you just experienced in your calling is an explosion, an invasion, and an overwhelming rush of the Infinite into your little world. The Holy has just swept you away in a tidal wave of purposeful grace. And now the seminary (and the denomination) wants you to sit in a classroom, read a book, follow the rules, jump through the hoops, graduate ... *and then,* maybe, if you're good and obedient, you can take one of the denominational sloops out on the water of God's grace for a bit of a run. The "Wow!" made you bold and daring enough to risk martyrdom among the micro-culture for which your heart bursts, and the seminary-denominational experience will make you timid and help you design a five-year incremental strategic plan that minimizes the risks.

It did not start out that way. There is quite a literature lamenting the demise of the true "university" that began in the medieval world as a fellowship of entrepreneurs questing after truth, and that was very different from the information factories we have created today. In the ancient or medieval worlds, anyone with an experience of "Wow!" was sent to a cave to wrestle with the devil and embrace Christ, then to a monastery to embrace the spiritual life ... *and then* shot into the world to feed the hungry, heal the sick, lead a crusade, launch a revolt, and live or die in the attempt.

Not so today. Denominations prefer, and seminaries train, knowledgeable, intelligent, reasonable, merciful, prophetic, manageable, controllable, officers of the church. The "Wow!" wavers. And the spiritually yearning, institutionally alienated public (those "gentiles" of the postmodern world) is disappointed.

E-mail #3
Subject: The Sources of Discontent

Dear Christian Companion:

Yes, I know that when you informed your pastor of your interest in ministry that she was jubilant. She is as happy for herself as she is for you, because she was able to recruit another to follow in her footsteps. And yes, I know that the judicatory was also jubilant. There is a desperate shortage of clergy in your denomination, and the judicatory is already pondering how they can use your gifts and talents to further the denomination's future.

Now, read that last sentence over again and see if it does not raise your anxieties! The primary reason congregations decline is that they look upon new members as a resource of talent and wealth that they can use to further *their* institutional agendas, rather than generously place all the assets of the church at the disposal of seekers so that they can find and fulfill their own destinies in God's mission field. The public knows that the church is out to "use" them, and is wary about joining the church! In exactly the same way, the primary reason denominations cannot recruit clergy is that they look upon candidates like yourself as a resource of talent and energy that they can deploy to further their institutional agendas, rather than place all the assets of the denomination and seminary at the disposal of the young apostle to discern her or his unique mission and pursue it. And candidates for ministry quickly figure this out . . . and leave.

You are jubilant. Your pastor is jubilant. The judicatory is jubilant. Yet I fear you are all jubilant for different reasons. Have you received the formal letter from your judicatory yet? Note the polite, yet distant, congratulations in the first paragraph. They are glad, but circumspect. They want you to know that their approval is all-important. They make no real promises, because you might have an aberrant psychological profile, or an ambiguous life history or sexual experience, or anomalous political views, or incorrect theological perspectives. Therefore, most of the letter outlines the timeline, requirements, and evaluation processes that you will need to pursue in order to graduate from seminary and be certified by the denomination.

Is your anxiety rising even more? On the face of it, the requirements listed are quite reasonable. After all, the denomination ("the company") does not really know you, and it makes sense that before they offer you a job that deals in sensitive human relations they should have confidence that you are not crazy, possessed of an unrepentant criminal record, a collector of child pornography, a closet Nazi, or a believer in human sacrifice. Nevertheless, there is something disturbing about the Christian church presuming you are guilty and demanding that you prove your innocence.

- First of all, one worries about the credibility of the judges: all those denominational officials, professors, and personnel committees, chosen by popular election and political appointment, and preserved in office by political maneuvering and academic tenure. They all have perspectives they hold dear and agendas to protect or pursue. They are all "servants of the system," but they also see themselves as "reformers of the system," and they all know you are a potential voting member of the denomination and future alumnus of the seminary.

They will more likely understand and accept your calling if it fits their agenda and leverages their vision of
reform.

• Second of all, one worries about the credibility of the
process: all that bureaucracy, meetings divorced from
ongoing relationship that will vote on your future,
examinations that purport to be objective but are all too
subjective. Your pastor who is so jubilant may in fact be
politically or theologically suspect in the senior management of "the company." Your sponsoring church
might be at the cutting edge of one faction or region,
but committees dominated by another faction or region
will make the decisions for your future. Since you can't
quantify a calling, how can a committee objectively
evaluate it?

Compare your reading of history and the daily newspaper with
the officious, rather overconfident letter you receive from the
judicatory. The truth is that if Justin Martyr, Origen, Augustine,
Calvin, Luther, and Wesley were candidates for ordained ministry
in your denomination, they probably would not pass the evaluation. And the truth is that, despite these overconfident requirements, criminals, child abusers, political extremists, and
theological idiots seem all too easily to get certified and ordained.

All this lies behind that seemingly reasonable, but highly
bureaucratic letter, that you are about to receive from a judicatory
eager to "use" you for its institutional purposes. Makes you pause,
doesn't it?

E-mail #4
Subject: The Growing Discontent

Dear Christian Companion:
Yeah, I guess I do sound cynical. I can feel your righteous
indignation as you write: "Now I understand why people say you
are anti-denominational!" But remember! I've been a pastor in and

out of political favor in three denominations and two countries, and a highly respected national denominational leader, and my own transition to cross-denominational consulting is one of the few that has happened in peaceful mutual respect. I add that I am one of the very few "church growth" types who possess, value, and apply an academic research doctoral degree in philosophical theology. I can say with some authority that "some of my best friends are denominational leaders and seminary academics"!

That is my point. People within the system, and people who had high credibility in the system and dropped out of the system, share all of the doubts about the system expressed in my earlier letter. These are not original with me. The public shares these doubts. The world shares these doubts. Church people share these doubts. An underground of seminary and denominational officialdom shares these doubts. But despite all this doubt, seminary and denominational powers-that-be still look incredulous and say, "Just trust us!"

My cynicism is not that denominational leaders or seminary professors are political creatures, or that they make imperfect judgments. So are we all, and so we all behave. My cynicism is that the rationale behind the very existence of denomination and seminary has shifted from empowering people to fulfill their calling to walk with Christ in mission to using people to protect and further an institutional church agenda. As soon as that fundamental shift happens, a church that is supposed to be based on trust and deep spirituality becomes a denomination based on accountability and institutional obedience. All the political limitations and imperfect decisions natural to the human condition are then multiplied, magnified, and mutated beyond the imagination and credibility of the spiritually hungry public.

There is a revolution coming, and it is led both from within the system and beyond the system. It is not a liberal revolution or a conservative revolution. It is simply a revolution led by cynical people who want to stop playing at institutional maintenance and start living a mission movement once again.

E-mail #5
Subject: The Changing Process

Dear Christian Companion:
Your post is full of questions: *What seminary should I attend? What curriculum should I study? Which professors will help me the most? What is the denominational process for ordination? Where do I apply? If the old training structures don't understand my call, how can they train me to pursue it effectively? Where do I go? How do I pursue this?* You really, really want to be in mission, but feel totally inadequate for the task. I suspect Priscilla and Aquila felt that way before you.

First and foremost, stop trying to fit into a "structure," and start looking for "partners." It used to be that "ministry candidates" could safely put themselves in the hands of a denominational certification process and a seminary training program, and the experts would guide them to obtain the knowledge and skills that they needed. Today's "mission movers" need to take responsibility themselves to customize the learning track for their own life context and mission goals. You need knowledge and skills that simply are not recognized, taught, or even on the "radar screen" of any single denomination or seminary.

Education for church leadership was so simple in the old days. You graduated from a liberal arts college, went through the certification hoops and hunkered down on-site in a seminary, and routed yourself into social service and health care or into the local congregation to preach, share sacraments, do philanthropic stuff, and counsel people.

Education for mission immersion is more chaotic. First your heart bursts to share Christ with a specific micro-culture. Then you look around for partners who can equip you to customize any tactic to do it. The primary partnerships are no longer seminaries and denominations, but relevant congregations, nonprofits, corporations, parachurches, business schools, social services, health care organizations, and literally anybody who shares your "heartburst" for a given micro-culture.

E-mail #6
Subject: More Potential Partnerships Than Ever Before

Dear Christian Companion:

I can sense your astonishment: *Are you saying that denominational certification and seminary training are irrelevant for contemporary Christian mission?*

Not irrelevant, but secondary. Seminaries and denominations that were once major players in the training and deployment of ministers are now minor players in the training and deployment of mission movers. They are useful to teach *some* subjects, train *some* skills, and broker *some* networks . . . but are no longer dominant partners.

I attach to this e-mail a couple of diagrams I use in teaching. The first diagram illustrates the partnership of the modern, Christendom world between denominational certification and seminary training.

The Partners: Old Christendom

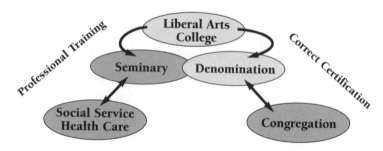

The "Patronage Game"

Students fresh out of liberal arts colleges followed parallel, interfaced tracks of certification and training, and ended up either in some form of faith-based social service or health care, or in a local parish. The system is designed to minimize competition and maximize patronage, so that, in the end, a call or appointment to an agency or parish has more to do with whom you know than *what* you know.

The second chart illustrates the complexity and diversity of partnership options today. Christian leaders are emerging later in life, from many professional backgrounds, in a variety of cultural contexts, and with less time and money to invest.

The Partners: Emerging Pagan World

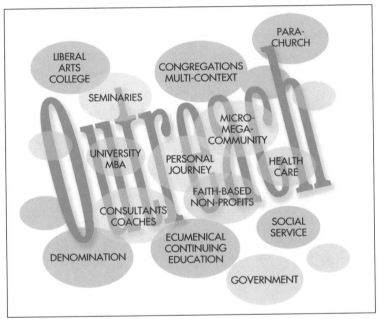

All these and more can be potential partners to train a Christian "mission mover," because all organizations now see themselves as "educational institutions." Research and development, constant cultural adaptation, and holistic health (including spirituality) are now primary organizational goals in the corporate and nonprofit sectors. A Christian CEO may run a business on Christian principles, with a clear goal to model Christian community among employees, and have more to offer for training a "mission mover" than any seminary, and more impact on society for Christian behavior than any parish church. In the pagan world, every organization is "spiritualized"—potentially sacred and missionally effective.

E-mail #7
Subject: The Fight for Methodological Control

Dear Christian Companion:

You are right to observe that when denominations and seminaries are placed in the context of this diversity of potential learning partners, their claims for *exclusive control* to educate church leadership smacks of unrealistic jealousy. So long as people wanted simply to be educated for church leadership, this exclusive control was possible. Now that more and more people are longing for mission immersion, it is no longer possible.

One reason that denominations and seminaries fight for exclusive control of the educational partnership is that they must protect their own bureaucracies and tenure tracks. If exclusive control is lost, bureaucracies and faculties will need to be reduced and guaranteed jobs will necessarily be subject to the competitive marketplace.

The deeper reason that denominations and seminaries fight for exclusive control of the educational partnership is that they are still obsessed with the protection of sacred space, sacred people, sacred time, and the resulting sacred harmony of the saints. Relevance and productivity are secondary. It is more important to them that you be a theologically pure alumnus, or a politically correct officer of the church, than a constantly adaptive, risk-taking missionary. That is the attitude North American industry had in the twentieth century and it darned near killed it.

The partnerships that are really going to focus and equip your Christian mission will be an eclectic, cross-disciplinary, and cross-cultural mix. In order to find your way, you will need a mentor and a team to find the help that you need most for the next step, not a core curriculum and course catalogue.

E-mail #8
Subject: Mentors

Dear Christian Companion:

You write: "I guess I always assumed that if I did go through the denominational certification process and seminary training, then I would find a mentor and a team. So where do I find a mentor and a team? For that matter, what the heck is a mentor and a team?"

A mentor is someone who speaks from his or her own experience of life struggle, spiritual victory, and constant growth to help you overcome adversity, discern hope, and customize a learning path. A true team is a small group that shares similar core values and beliefs, celebrates an enthusiasm for a mission, eagerly interfaces their skills to achieve that mission, and seriously holds one another accountable for the fruits of the mission.

Where to find them? You have to be willing to *search* . . . to search *prayerfully* . . . and to search *in unlikely places*. Like most providential happenings, finding mentors and teams requires diligent work, but success usually feels serendipitous because you found these people in cultures, careers, or lifestyles where you least expected to find them. In a recent post I mentioned Priscilla and Aquila. They became missionaries only after being mentored by Paul and Silas, and later encountered Apollos on the road and became mentors to him.

When universities and seminaries were originally born out of the libraries, scriptoriums, and spiritual disciplines of the monasteries, they were indeed places where avid missionaries could find mentors and teams. Unfortunately, modernity has made universities (and seminaries!) into factories that produce skilled laborers, or into rehabilitation clinics that recycle dysfunctional people. They are no longer places to find mentors and teams, but places to find technicians and therapy groups. If you are looking for a mentor, I suggest starting with the manager of Mail Boxes Etc. who once offered you a job. Maybe God is in that.

E-mail #9
Subject: The Mutually Mentoring Team

Dear Christian Companion:

Well, I don't blame you for being skeptical. When I say, "Maybe the key mentor for your personal growth might be the manager at Mail Boxes Etc.," you reply with "You can't be serious!" This is the modern myth of "professionalism" getting in the way. I explained somewhere (in my book *Coaching Change,* I think) that at least in the sphere of religion, the importance of professionals to guide your path and teach you skills is radically diminished. In the fast-changing cultures and the bubbling cauldron of spirituality we experience today, we are entering a new world of amateurs. Everybody is incompetent. Everybody is inadequate.

Don't let a Ph.D. fool you. They are just as amateur as you are in the emerging pagan world. Of course the Ph.D. may have *knowledge* (i.e., "information") that you need, and perhaps experience (i.e., "skills") that may still be relevant. That was sufficient in the Christendom world. A good many clergy could get by with knowledge and skills. Today, however, you need wisdom (the intuition to apply knowledge) and *adaptability* (the ability to innovate tactics). Behind all of this you need *a deep connection with Jesus and his mission* more than knowledge about Christianity.

Consider the early missionaries to the "gentiles" from the New Testament. Yes, Paul at least studied with the Pharisees about faith, history, and religious practice. Even that cannot be compared to seminary classrooms, of course. My point is that he discarded a lot of what he learned, and rarely spoke of the rest. Instead, you see him consulting with Luke and Onesimus, traveling with a companionship, and interacting with the apostles—none of whom graduated from high school (well, maybe Levi the tax collector did a community college course in accounting). This is the mutually mentoring team—the network of spiritual amateurs—with whom he remained in contact all of his life.

From ancient perspective, this is your first step to prepare for ministry. The first step is not choosing a seminary. It is choosing a mutually mentoring team. This team of wise, adaptable people passionate about Jesus and his mission is the companionship with which you will network all your life. Ancient and medieval missionaries never entered ministry on their own. They did it in a team. If they did not have one, they joined a monastery or a nunnery in order to find one. Then, maybe, they went to seminary.

E-mail #10
Subject: Monasticism as the Inheritor of the Mission Spirit

Dear [Anxious] Christian Companion:
"My God! You want me to enter a nunnery!" I am sorry that you are questioning my sanity, but then again, I do too at times. Just as the modern church has addicted you to professionalism, so also it has deceived you about the role of the ancient monastic movement. You have been told that the monastery and nunnery were vehicles to retreat from the real world, and, by contrast, the parish church and seminary were the vehicles to minister to the real world. Such rubbish! In fact, the great missionary and reforming movements (Celtic, Latin, and Greek) all originated from monasteries and nunneries, and were primarily led by monks and nuns. Even the Wesleyan reform originated from class meetings of laity rather than ordained priests. It was the monastic movement that really inherited the "mission to the gentiles." The seminary trained clergy hunkered down among the already faithful and built cathedrals on five acres of land beside the expressway.

The monastic movement was founded upon a companionship of mutually mentoring teams. If they seemed to "retreat" from the world, it was because the *real* world was a struggle between the temptations of the devil and true union with God. Once they addressed that "real world," they reentered the "illusory world" to help others make it more like the realm of God. The mission spirit never died or became secondary as it did in the established parish ministry. It never became an "outreach program" of the church. It remained the core of Christian experience.

Church leaders, from the early papacy to the Protestant Reformation to the array of modern denominations, have always been antagonistic to the monastic movement. They wanted to educate people for church leadership, and the monks and nuns wanted to educate people for mission immersion. The former required professionals with knowledge and skills who loved the church. The latter required amateurs with wisdom and adaptability who loved being with Jesus.

Actually, I think this has been a helpful digression. I hope this has given you the inkling that there is a very different method of learning involved in training people for mission immersion. This methodology is not really a contemporary innovation (contrasting with the "traditional" approach of seminaries and certifications). In fact, this different method IS the "traditional" way, with ancient roots going all the way back to the mission to the gentiles and the emergence of the monastic movement in the fourth century.

The Emerging Learning Methodology

E-mail #11
Subject: Beyond Literacy

Dear Christian Companion:

I appreciate your aggressiveness in challenging me. That is part of how you relate to mentors. You write: "I'll have to come back to the question of where I am going to find this mentoring! Right now, though, I have to challenge your seeming denigration of a basic theological curriculum in preparation for ministry. Personally, I really feel a need for some fundamental education in Scripture, history, theology, and missiology. I hate to admit it, but what I don't know would fill volumes!"

Believe me, I understand that and appreciate your humility. Certainly there are subjects you should study for faithful, high-integrity, Christian mission. My point is that even after you graduate from seminary and are certified by a denomination, what you don't know will fill even more volumes. During your seclusion in the classroom, the world will have moved light years in umpteen new directions, and a zillion new micro-cultures will have emerged that you still don't know how to reach with Christ.

The more important issue is not the content of your education, but the methodology in which you will constantly learn. Back in the old days, when seminaries and denominations worked well, content was crucial and methodology was secondary. The universally accepted learning method was to sit in a classroom, listen to an expert, read a book, and follow the curriculum. There was only one symbol-system you had to master in order to learn anything from systematic theology to brain surgery. All that mattered was content.

No more. It's not that people are post-literate, but that they are omni-literate. Sometimes they learn in linear fashion reading a book. Most often they learn in lateral fashion by experiencing a data byte, or viewing a movie, or experimenting with a new idea, or conversing with a friend or stranger, or interacting with a new micro-culture. It happens in life, not in class. It happens with a peer group, not an expert. The ability to learn from multiple medias all at once means that even book-based learning will never be the same. People trained to read e-mail are inevitably disappointed with a mere book. No hyperlinks embedded in each paragraph to carry you instantly to another media or another world!

Traditional linear, classroom, seminary education, like all education in all subjects, is being outpaced by the postmodern world. The day after you learned the skill, the world changed and it won't work anymore. And the afternoon after you thought you learned the truth, the perspective changed and it doesn't interpret reality anymore. Learning today happens *after* failure, not *before* risk. In happens in immersion, not in retreat. The truth is you may never know much in advance *what* you need to learn to be in mission with Jesus. The best you can do is train yourself *how* to learn constantly with Jesus.

The biggest challenge of all—for you, for the church, and for anyone who has grown up in a culture dominated by public education and the philosophy of John Dewey—is that curriculum-based learning has given way to talisman-based learning. A talisman is an image, data byte, video clip, song, or devotional object around which people organize their learning. A talisman is a two-way connection with the infinite. It is a symbol, in that it reminds us of eternal truths. More than this, it is also a portal through which the infinite tugs at our heart and sustains us through the dark night. Spiritual growth is no longer organized around a Bible study in the parlor, but around the dangly thing from the rearview mirror, the screensaver on the computer, or the devotional object around your neck.

E-mail #12
Subject: What about My Books?

Dear Christian Companion:

Well, you've got me there! You write: "I understood that you have an academic research doctorate in philosophical theology and used to teach in seminary. And you write all of these books, clearly expecting somebody is going to read them. Are you turning your back on all of that?"

No, I am not. Why do you think I travel constantly, rather than remain in a seminary classroom? Why do I try to use various media to create a learning environment? Why would I rather choreograph an experience than preach a sermon? I am recognizing that "lecture" and "book" are increasingly less significant for the learning experience. It's all in the cross-cultural experience, the conversations, the images and sounds and smells and touching.

It is more important to the mission of Jesus that Christian leaders know how to think than accumulate a library of information. It is more important that they learn how to synthesize new things than memorize old things. It is more important that they speak HTML, paint pictures, compose songs, and think in metaphors than read grammatically correct English and manipulate parliamentary procedure.

In an omni-literate world, people learn like they did in the pre-literate world of the earliest church and medieval times.

Remember Chaucer's *Canterbury Tales*? You read it in high school. That's how people learn today. They don't enroll in a degree program, live in a dormitory, attend a classroom, read books, and pass examinations. Instead, they burn tattoos into their flesh, join a pilgrim band, and start walking through culture. Chaucer's pilgrims couldn't read. They did carry talismans. I saw one in a museum: prayer beads, carved in wood, each about the size of a golf ball, and hinged. Open the bead, and see a tableau of the annunciation, or crucifixion, or the trials of a saint particularly relevant to your life situation. Feel the Infinite touch your heart through the portal. Listen to a mentor. Give alms to the starving masses beside the road. Share the stories of life struggle and spiritual victory with your companions along the way.

In the old days you learned one book at a time, one course at a time, or one academic degree program at a time. Now you learn one conversation at a time, one micro-culture at a time, and one unsettling experience at a time.

E-mail #13
Subject: Sorry to Offend ... *NOT!*

Dear [Angry] Christian Companion:

In the midst of your long rant, the following excerpt deserves a response before you cease our e-mail correspondence: "You're crazy, you know. As my grandmother would say, you're 'crazier than a hoot owl.' I came to you wondering if I should go to seminary, and you tell me I should go on pilgrimage. Sure, I read Chaucer in high school ... and hated every minute of it. Somehow I don't think wearing prayer beads and joining a pilgrim band are going to help me lead a church in rural North Dakota, urban Philadelphia, or remote Newfoundland. Thanks for nothing!"

You hated *reading* Chaucer. Just like in seminary you will hate *reading* Justin Martyr. You would better enjoy Chaucer as drama ... and imagine what it would be like to *be* Chaucer—really doing those things, and interacting with those people, and traveling on that path?

Wake up, friend! Learning like Chaucer in the pre-literate world is *exactly* how people in rural North Dakota, urban Philadelphia, and remote Newfoundland are doing it today, no matter what their economic, ethnic, or language status. One big reason public education and traditional churches are struggling and dying today is that they refuse to face that fact.

Sorry to offend you. I thought you wanted to be an effective "bringer of the gospel" to the real world. Apparently you want to be an effective "bringer of the gospel" to the imaginary world constructed out of the perspective of so-called "higher education."

The most important reason I urge you to emulate Chaucer's characters is that pilgrims risk everything they have to arrive at a holy destination. Modern people and career clergy do not do this. They risk only 40-60 hours of work and a percentage of their income not already invested in the pension plan to arrive … where? A denominational annual meeting? A bigger, more prestigious pulpit? Harry Emerson Fosdick's church as it was in the 1940s? A just society implementing public policies that will be in favor until the next election? An Easter Vigil marked by perfect liturgy and the powerful singing of Handel's *Messiah*? I find more and more traditionally trained and certified clergy facing a mid-mission crisis and asking, *Why? What's the point? Where is all this taking me, and do I really want to go there?*

What is your "holy destination"? Figure that out, and then decide on what learning methodology will get you there. The learning methodology you choose will reveal the *true* destination of your heart.

E-mail #14
Subject: Holy Destination

Dear [Angry] Christian Companion:
Apparently you have misunderstood me. I ask you about your "holy destination," and you reply by describing some kind of

"journey" that "leads into mystery," but that allows you to meet many people "along the way." You also add some sort of garbage about how in the end the "journey is the destination" and all that matters is appreciating the journey. What a load of modern crap! I have met more burned-out, disillusioned, cynical, and abused clergy who profess that stuff than I care to list.

God does not call you to be on a journey, but to be on a mission. The road to mission is not a journey of endless fascination. It is a dusty, dangerous, onerous, necessary evil that any sane person and any intelligent Christian would prefer to avoid ... *except that God has called them down that road for the express purpose of getting somewhere, communicating with some micro-culture, starting a faith community in some new location, and joining Jesus, who is waiting for you to catch up.*

This is the difference between education for church leadership and education for mission immersion. Education for church leadership assumes that the gospel is already the norm of culture, and that the pagan world has largely been tamed, and all you need to do is explore the hidden corners of the garden. You follow the stepping-stones of the Christian year and ponder the three-year cycle of the Common Lectionary. Education for mission immersion assumes the Gospel is an intrusion on an alien world—that those who bring it are placing themselves at great risk, and that one must be highly motivated to dare to travel. The stepping-stones were laid by some Roman legion and you have to connect Scripture with the indigenous culture.

If you do not have a destination in mind, you will never make the journey. In medieval times, 50 percent of the pilgrims never made it to their destination. Most of them died along the way from exposure, starvation, bandits, war, or accident. Some of them decided the goal wasn't worth it and stopped to build an inn, plunder a village, or sell computers. The ones that made it often never returned home, because the *destination* was better than their place of origin and the journey itself held no interest.

So I repeat: *What is your holy destination?* What great goal and overarching purpose motivates your travels? When all is said and done, where do you want to get to, who do you want to be with, why do you want to go there, and what in heaven's name do you hope to accomplish?

E-mail #15
Subject: Your Holy Destination

Dear Christian Companion:

Sooooo . . . you urgently, desperately, passionately want to help the urban populations of America connect with Jesus Christ so they can experience and build total personal and social health. Why didn't you say so in the first place? It sounds like a great goal to which to surrender your life. It sounds like God would want that very much. It is a destination that does seem truly "holy." Why did you bother sidetracking yourself into all that guff about the value of the "journey," when all along you had no desire to stop and smell the roses if it delayed you in achieving your life ambition?

Amazing, isn't it, how clarity about your personal mission helps you focus on the content and method of your learning.

The content of learning we will talk about shortly, but probably you are aware that you will need to learn Spanish, appreciate strong coffee, experience racism, study the justice and social service systems, understand the power of charismatic renewal, and acquire the ability to talk about faith in street language. You may begin wondering just how those core curriculum classes on expository preaching, denominational polity, and ancient Greek and Hebrew are going to help you.

But it is the methodology of learning that is more important. If the urban populations are your mission target, then you need to think as they do, value indigenous culture as they do, and learn as they do. You need to "go native" to reach the "natives," not to change them from their "native ways" but to communicate the gospel and the vision of mission through their "native ways."

E-mail #16
Subject: A Typology of Learning

Dear Christian Companion:

Perhaps I misled you in my previous post with my rather glib references to the content and method of learning implied by "going native." You leap to the conclusion that I am simply talking about "techniques," and therefore fear that by understanding a different learning methodology you will simply be learning how to manipulate people.

Perhaps a short lesson in cultural history is in order. One of the early innovations in aviation was introduced by a WWI German pilot named Immelman. He invented a high-speed loop, with a twist, that could allow a plane to return to the same course but reverse its relative position in relationship to other aircraft. Something of a "cultural Immelman" has occurred in western civilization.

The attached chart is extremely general, and no doubt there are enormous variations in date, region, and ethnicity. Nevertheless, it helps us understand that a learning methodology is not a technique, but a wholly unconscious habit of reflection about truth that is shaped by culture itself. It is not "truth" that is relative, but the methods that people of various cultures use to reflect on "truth." Learning methodologies evolve as culture evolves, and while at any given time there may be an anomaly like Erasmus, whose erudition contrasted with both Reformation and Counter-Reformation, or Newton, whose deductive rationality contrasted with the speculative natural philosophy of his time, the people of a culture generally reflect on truth in a certain way.

This evolution or relativity of the culture of learning is the reason it is so silly for people of one era or culture to look so condescendingly upon people of another era or culture. There is no real justification for modern, scientific people to dismiss the perspective on truth of medieval people as "superstitious" or "stupid," or for literate university graduates to dismiss the profundity of illiterate, uneducated people . . . and vice versa.

Period	Culture of Learning	Experience
9th–14th Centuries	Pre-Literate Society of Symbolic Tribes Monastery and Nunnery	Few read and only in non-indigenous languages; icon, image, and devotional objects ground reflection.
15th–17th Centuries	An Early Literate Society of Privileged Classes Endowed Universities and Colleges	The printing press makes reading available to those who can afford it, and abstract linear thinking grows in popularity.
17th–18th Centuries	A Literate Society of Independent Nations Liberal Arts Universities and Colleges	Deductive reasoning flourishes in a matrix of external relations, in which objects, individuals, and nations collide and interact.
19th–20th Centuries	A Literate Society of Educated Consumers Denominational Colleges and Applied Sciences	Industrial expansion raises technological innovation over the liberal arts, reducing humanity to measurable traits.
1900–1950s	A Scientific Society of Educated Researchers Specialized Institutes	Quantum theory and inductive reasoning promise to make life easier, wealthier, and healthier.

1950s–1980s	An Omni-Literate Society of Privileged Corporations Corporate Specialized Training	Computer language, Internet, and multi-national economics render truth increasingly abstract and quantifiable.
1980s–1990s	A Cross-Cultural Society of Macro-Literate Networks Long Distance Learning	The spread of information and migration of global populations unfolds in a matrix of internal relations in which all things are internally related to other things.
1990s–2000	A Cross-Cultural Society of Micro-Literate Lifestyles Global Apprenticeships	Cultural forms blend and interact, forming micro-cultures with their own special interests, symbols, and language.
2000 and Beyond	An Omni-Symbolic Society of Post-Literate Tribes Small Group Interaction and Mentoring	Talisman (symbol, image) replaces or interfaces with abstract concepts, becoming the fulcrum of meaning for self-defined cells, small groups, and networks.

I am less concerned here about precision timelines and cultural details than I am to demonstrate how learning methodology changes both the way we think and, ultimately, how we reflect on "truth." This is a "cultural Immelman." It's not that the postmodern world has simply "returned" to the ancient world. Along the way there has been a "twist," so that the learning methodologies of the interim have been morphed and moved and incorporated into something new.

E-mail #17
Subject: Where Are Today's Universities and Seminaries?

Dear Christian Companion:

Thank you for this question. You are discerning that universities and seminaries usually think of themselves as more cutting-edge than they really are. This was OK when the world changed slowly, but increasingly unacceptable as the world moves faster. In my view, most of the universities, seminaries, or theological colleges assume a culture of learning somewhere between the mid-nineteenth century and the early 1980s.

- A few of the most fundamentalist ones assume the world is still a "literate society of independent nations," and tend to confuse national identity and religious truth, so that mission and colonialism blend together.
- Most of the practical seminaries training people for ordination assume the world is still "a literate society of educated consumers," and they treat the curriculum like an applied science to train clergy "engineers" who can construct a functional religious institution.
- Most of the university faculties of religious studies and some prestigious seminaries assume the world is still a "scientific society of educated researchers," and approach religion through sociology, political science, psychology, or other more quantifiable disciplines.

• A few seminaries and theological colleges have broken into the learning culture of the 1980s (an "omni-literate society of privileged corporations"), and have begun to interface theological education with business schools or other degree programs and initiate multi-campus or long-distance learning.

Generally speaking, however, universities and seminaries do not really understand the emerging, talisman-based, tribal culture of learning. When you graduate from any of these institutions, you will unwittingly carry their assumptions with you and pay the price of irrelevance in ministry.

E-mail #18
Subject: The Importance of Method

Dear Christian Companion:
Sorry to confuse you by drawing such a large and abstract picture. Nothing like a message from your companion ("What the heck are you talking about?") to bring you back down to earth.
My point is that in different eras, and among different cultures, people acquire knowledge and gain insight in different ways. Academics and North Americans who have grown up in a public education system based on scientific principles and the philosophy of John Dewey tend to assume that there is only one good way to learn. Before you can teach anyone anything, you first must teach them how to learn the right way. The problem is that teaching people how to learn prejudices what they will learn.
For example, when the pastor assumes that the best way to learn is through listening to expository sermons, reading curriculums, and studying concepts in the seclusion of the church parlor, it is no big surprise that what people end up learning is rational dogma, institutional obedience, and a condescending attitude toward outsiders. Sure, they may learn some good stuff about the Bible, history, theology, and human behavior along the way ... but a hidden selectivity in the learning method will

choose certain verses, stories, ideas, and habits as superior to others. Isn't it surprising how seminary-educated pastors and poorly educated urbanites can all read about Bible, history, theology, and human behavior and barely have anything in common to talk about? Usually the pastor says: "What I want to talk about is more important than what you want to talk about, and my way of learning is better than your way of learning." In the old days (circa 1950), people replied: "Golly gee, we must be really stupid, please help us." Today (circa 2004), people reply: "The pastor must be really stupid, how can we help her?"

E-mail #19
Subject: A Comparison of Methods

Dear Christian Companion:
Yes, you are beginning to get it. Three or more years from now, when you finish seminary and are deployed in some church, which response will be the real response of people to your ministry?

There is still a generation or so that still values the learning methodology in which you have been indoctrinated. They get mad about *what* you preach and teach, but they will never doubt the correctness of *how* you preach and teach and your credibility to do so. However, more and more generations might be willing to talk about *what* you think, but they can no longer connect with *how* you learn and communicate or the *priorities* that seem to surface from your (to them) extraordinarily odd way of thinking. They do doubt your credibility. The relevance of a pastor today to one-sixteenth of the population, and the irrelevance of the pastor to fifteen-sixteenths of the population has more to do with *how* you learn and communicate than with *what* you learn and communicate. It's the proverbial "ships passing in the night."

Attached is a comparison of methods I use in visual presentations.

The Learning Methodology

Modern	**Postmodern**
• Classroom	• Action Reflection
• Curriculum	• Image and Sound and Data Byte
• Teacher	• Mentor and Coach
• Linear by "Subject"	• Lateral by "Issue"
• Passive	• Interactive
• Solo	• Team-based Cohort
• Add-on to Schedule	• Blended into Lifestyle
• Uniform, Transferable	• Contextual, Customized
• Traditional Technology	• Indigenous, Contemporary Technology
• Face-to-face	• Face-to-face AND Web-based
• Class Size	• Compatible Companions

As you compare, return to my original image from Chaucer's *Tales* of the pilgrim band journeying down the road to its holy destination. That is the postmodern culture of learning, which is a kind of twisted return to ancient experience: "An Omni-Symbolic Society of Post-Literate Tribes."

E-mail #20
Subject: The Learning Context

Dear Christian Companion:
That's right! Now you begin to understand why you hate class-rooms, lectures, campuses, residential dormitories, and inflexible course curriculums! It's because that is no longer your natural

learning context. You like environments, interaction, mobility, and choices. You learn best when you can ride your own horse, choose your own path, and generally blend your lifestyle into the learning experience. Chaucer's pilgrim band simply will not tolerate a traditional learning context, not simply because it is uncomfortable, but because it is ineffective.

Now translate that to a future church you have supposedly been trained to lead. If you hate classrooms, lectures, campuses, residential dormitories, and inflexible curriculums . . . why would you imagine the people with whom you are in mission will like sanctuaries, sermons, church properties, liturgies, and pews?

E-mail #21
Subject: The Relational Web

Dear Christian Companion:
Right again! Chaucer's pilgrims traveled in a small peer group, enjoyed mutual mentoring, sought and received coaching when they needed and as they needed it, and interacted with cross-cultural diversity along the way. Again, that is what you enjoy, and it is how you have learned the most.

Translate that to a future church you have supposedly been trained to lead. If you are skeptical of certified professionals who neither seek nor sustain long-term trusting relationships that run holistically through their lifestyles . . . why should people within and beyond your church trust you?

E-mail #22
Subject: The Symbol System

Dear Christian Companion:
Yes, this is the hardest thing. It is difficult for the modern person to surrender abstract concepts and linear thinking as the only, or even best, vehicle to truth. It is hard for us to understand how

an image, symbol, object, data byte, video clip, or song can in fact teach more, reveal more, communicate more than mere words and sentences and sermons. Yet they do. And these various images, sounds, smells, tastes, and feelings form networks or experiences of communication that convict, convince, instruct, and motivate more powerfully than anything Gutenberg could ever have imagined through the printing press.

Why do you think the really big church fights today are over music, stained glass windows, objects on the altar, images projected on the wall, and even the scent of the sanctuary or taste of the wine? Nobody argues over what you preach, pray, read, or recite anymore. Heavens, nobody bothers to listen to the sermon anymore, and if they do they mishear or misunderstand it anyway. Say anything with a smile and follow it up with a firm handshake, and you can preach pretty much whatever you want. Words do not reveal the truth today. The symbols and images and sounds and smells with which we surround ourselves reveal more than abstractions.

E-mail #23
Subject: The Portal System

Dear Christian Companion:
My dear Holmes, you amaze me! You actually went back to my past e-mails to reflect on what I said about the inability of denominations and seminaries to acknowledge the apocalyptic "Wow!" experience that is your calling. Maybe I should collect our e-mail correspondence into an e-book.

The power of the emerging learning methodology is that it is more than a symbol system. It is a portal system. It is a network of images, sounds, tastes, or data bytes that form a network of portals through which the infinite reaches our lives (heart, mind, body, soul) and then twists, upturns, overwhelms, redirects, and reshapes our living. The limit of power for abstraction is to be prophetic. But the power of talisman is apocalyptic. It is as much about "Wow!" as it is about "who, what, when, or why."

One might argue that the end result of a merely literate society (the modern world) is chronic relativism. Abstractions become interpreted in any number of ways and contexts, and no one is better than another, because knowing is a game of competing symbol systems. The pre-literate and omni-literate societies know better. There is an absolute truth that interprets us. We experience it through a portal system, rather than through a symbol system. Our symbols become God's portals. Yet, as my mentor Paul Tillich implied, the infinite will simultaneously employ and shatter whatever symbol is used as portal. It becomes a memory, a shadow on the wall of Plato's cave that is more significant to humankind than a geological survey of the rock itself.

E-mail #24
Subject: Can We Tolerate Competing Learning Methodologies Any Longer?

Dear Christian Companion:
You have begun to discover the difference between how you believe you *ought* to learn and how you *really* learn. In a sense, modern universities and academicians have made a living off this distinction for a long time. Authoritative experts could impose a supposed discipline to thinking, and ignore the fact that your thinking was already "disciplined" but in a different manner than they wished. So in order to even approach theological education, the student needed to "unlearn" or "ignore" one methodology and "learn" or "adopt" an alternative.

In bygone days, life moved slowly enough to allow two distinct learning methodologies to occupy one person's attention at the same time. People could enter university or seminary and manage the transitional stress of acquiring a foreign learning methodology . . . and after they left seminary they could manage the subsequent transitional stress of reacquiring their old methodology still latent in their psyche. How many times I have counseled first-year sem-inarians frustrated by the linear, classroom expectations for abstraction demanded in the seminary . . . and how many times I have counseled seminary graduates frustrated that the linear, classroom expectations for abstraction didn't translate back in the real world of their parish. As long as life moved slowly enough, the stress was bearable. Then IBM introduced the personal computer in 1981, the Internet exploded, whole populations migrated, and the wireless economy took off. Today you can no longer afford the luxury of two competing learning methods.

E-mail #25
Subject: The Powers That Be

Dear Christian Companion:

How naïve can you get? "So why don't seminaries just change the way they teach?" What a thing to say! You see, behind the modern learning methodology is a huge structure of power and control. The institution, the tenure track, the salaries, the prestige, the very economic and political structure of the modern educational system is tied to the linear learning method that is disappearing. Linear learning is more easily controlled than talisman learning. That's why institutions prefer it. Linear learning gives rise to redundant levels of management that measure out, oversee, and generally control ideas. If you once recognize that people actually *learn* differently, and that they can no longer be cajoled and persuaded to *think* differently, academic careers are at stake. Whole curriculums become rubbish. Whole institutions become unnecessary. Jobs are lost.

Certainly there are visionaries within "the academy" who are willing to explore the reemerging pre-modern (now postmodern) learning methodology, and who are willing to stake their tenure track, pension plan, and academic prestige to do so. You will want to seek them out. Perhaps they have even made some headway to turn the dreadnought of the institution a few degrees to port. Their fate may be that of Origen, Abelard, and Erasmus.

The Content of Education

E-mail #26
Subject: Beyond Methodology: What Subjects Should You Study?

Dear Christian Companion:

Sorry for my outburst of pessimism ... sometimes it gets the better of me, and I accept your mild rebuke to get me back on track.

You write: "OK. I think I get the importance of method over content. The truth is, I wouldn't even be thinking about Christian ministry now if it weren't for the fact that I listened less to the sermon and liturgy, and I engaged more in conversations, cultures, medias, and experiments. But having accepted all that, isn't there still a core content of education that is an essential foundation for mission today? What should I study to begin it all?"

Yes, there is a content, but it is a different content than is taught by most seminaries or appreciated by most denominations.

- Biblical studies are absolutely crucial, but the focus, method, and application have shifted. The focus is less on historical accuracy, and more on mission application. The method is less scientific, and more metaphorical. The application has less to do with knowing the truth, and more to do with living the truth. In a nutshell, it has more to do with the allegorical method of Jerome and Gregory of Nyssa than the higher criticism of Bultmann or the Jesus Seminar.

- The field of historical studies is crucial, but the primary referent has changed. Instead of concentrating on late Christian history, especially the Reformation, Vatican II, and the civil rights crusade, now it concentrates on early Christian history, especially the earliest church, the martyrdom of Polycarp, and Celtic Christianity. And instead of church development in the European west, it refers to church development in the non-European east, south, and north.

- Systematic theology has given way to contextually developed Christologies, and because of this, missiology has replaced ecclesiology as the foundation of education for leadership. An in-depth understanding of other religions is important, but from the standpoint of mission dialogue rather than abstract theological debate ... and the "religions" included in the conversation have multiplied exponentially as the pagan world unfolds.

These are just highlights, but I think you can guess that such a shift is uncomfortable at best for established seminaries and denominations. In my capacity of a national denominational leader, I was once approached by a refugee Methodist pastor from Africa. He had fled to Canada, drove a taxi in the city, and spontaneously grown a church. Now he was seeking admittance for himself and his congregation into my denomination. Despite the rhetoric of "inclusiveness," denominational leaders insisted he leave his church, go into debt, and take courses at the local seminary in biblical higher criticism, European church music and liturgical practices, and theologies about everything from women to the environment. What did he do? He shook his head and walked away in disgust, continued to drive his cab, tripled worship attendance in two years, and multiplied mission impact beyond the imagination of most of the established churches in the area.

E-mail #27
Subject: Why There Still Needs to Be a "Core Database"

Dear Christian Companion:
I can well understand how your heart would go out to this pastor—and that you might be more excited about apprenticing yourself to that pastor than going back to the seminary classroom. Although it may seem like I am reversing my own position, however, I need to say that this would be a mistake.

The content of a "core curriculum" may have changed as Christians train for "missional movement" instead of being educated for "church leadership," but there is still a core database that you had better take time to learn. This is why monastic leaders would gather their disciples in the desert or lead them into seclusion for months or years on end. There is a core, and it must be learned, or the leader of the mission movement will find himself or herself cornered by ambiguity and unable to find the way forward.

Leaders in the missional movement will be more preoccupied with issues of integrity than leaders of institutional churches ever were. Church leaders worry about whether to serve communion by intinction or shot glass, but mission leaders have to worry about discerning the authentic Jesus amid competing spiritualities. Church leaders worry about proper baptism rites; mission leaders have to worry about interpreting the significance of unexpected and astonishing grace. Church leaders worry about the truth of Scripture; mission leaders worry about the truth in Scripture. Church leaders worry about continuity with the past; mission leaders worry about where Jesus will be fifteen years down the road in their zip code and how much they are willing to stake to meet up with him there.

E-mail #28
Subject: Stop Blaming Constantine!

Dear Christian Companion:
I appreciate your zeal to reject institutionalism and dogmatism in favor of mission and dialogue, but please, please stop talking about "pre-Constantinian" and "post-Constantinian" theology. Such vague stabs at interpreting the relevance of church history for postmodern mission reveal precisely why you should *not* go chasing off to apprentice yourself to that passionate African Methodist pastor in Canada. You lack precision. You lack clarity. You lack focus. And while a seminary may be only the best choice

in a list of poor options, at least you can choose the appropriate subjects for the missional movement and skip the others.

The historical period you need to study is *not* defined by the reign of Constantine. Contrary to popular opinion, Constantine did not legalize Christianity. He merely decided to tolerate it, or, better still, he legitimized the place of Christianity in formal dialogue with other religions. Later emperors would make Christianity the sole religion of the state, but when the cross appeared stamped on Roman coinage in 314 it was illustrated right beside the traditional pagan symbols of *Sol Invictus* and *Mars Conservator*. Constantine remained the *pontifex maximus* of the pagan state cult.

The real historical benchmark around which you shape your learning is A.D. 1054, the date of what became known as the "Great Schism" between the Western and Eastern churches that has not been healed to this day. The schism was precipitated by the refusal of the Eastern patriarchies to acknowledge the jurisdiction of Rome over their spiritual lives.

This "turning inward" of the church marks the real emergence of "Christendom." The energy of its spiritual leaders became focused on ecclesiology rather than missiology—control instead of witness. Prior to 1054, cross-cultural and religious dialogue not only was tolerated, but even encouraged. Entire nations and tribes converted, monastic movements multiplied, the nature and purpose of Jesus was explored, and faith was tested against the darkest times. After 1054, church leaders fought among themselves for power, scholasticism defined how many angels could dance on the head of a pin, crusades were launched, and the parish was unified and purified by polity.

E-mail #29
Subject: Stop Obsessing about the Reformation!

Dear Christian Companion:
As long as I am in a petulant mood, let me say that I wish you would stop sprinkling your e-mails with references to Luther,

Calvin, Knox, and Wesley. Christian modernity has shaped itself around the theological categories and issues of the Reformation; postmodern experience is too much like that of earliest times. It is not that the great conflicts between Protestantism and Roman Catholicism, or between Reformation and Counter-Reformation, or between this sect or denomination and that sect or denomination are unimportant. They are simply irrelevant to postmodern people who live in pagan, not Christendom, times. Attached is a chart that takes a fresh look at church history, and hopefully gives you an idea of what periods of history are most important for you to study to prepare yourself for today's mission field.

Period	Approximate Years	Description
Formation of the Core Database	1st–2nd centuries	Formation of the New Testament, the church as counter-culture, and apostolic schools of thought.
High Dialogical Period	3rd–5th centuries culminating in the Council of Nicaea in 325 and Chalcedon in 451	The quest for orthodoxy, the key questions about Jesus' nature and purpose, the persuasion of pagan culture, the beginnings of monasticism.
Low Dialogical Period	5th–11th centuries culminating in the Great Schism of 1054	The rise of monasticism, testing the faith in turbulent economic and political upheaval.

High Dogmatic Period	12th–16th centuries	The emergence of scholasticism, consolidation of political power, institutionalization, and institutional reform.
Low Dogmatic Period	16th–18th centuries	Fragmentation of church polities, competition with rising rationalism and humanism.
Cultural Accommodation	18th–20th centuries	Colonial and ideological agendas, conversion of institutional church to pagan expectations.

Basically, you want to take as many seminary courses as possible in the first three periods of church history, and only a few courses in the other periods. I am not trying to belittle the learning from the other periods. If you wanted to be educated for church leadership, these later periods would be crucial. As it is, they are only moderately helpful if you want to be educated for mission immersion.

E-mail #30
Subject: A Further Explanation

Dear Christian Companion:
I am glad we agree at least on the importance of studying the first period of history, the core database. The biblical foundation is crucial. However, please do not limit yourself to reading the canonical New Testament alone ... be sure to read the other Christian literature from this period as well.

As I suggested earlier, the *very worst way* to frame your histori-cal study is in pre- and post-Constantinian categories. Not only are the key dates all screwed up, but you have imposed a *political* template of discernment on a *religious* conversation. That is a very "modern" thing to do!

The better strategy is to divide your studies between the ante-Nicene Christian authors and the post-Nicene Christian authors (roughly corresponding to what I describe as the "high" and "low" dialogical periods). The first group includes people like Justin Martyr, Tertullian, Basil, and Jerome. All the debates over ortho-doxy then are relevant today, and none more so than the debate between Arius and Athanasius on the unity of God the Father and Son.

This is not mere abstraction. What hinged on the debate were our very expectations for salvation (including social justice, final personal vindication, ultimate forgiveness, and prospects for eter-nal bliss). The choice was (and is) this: Is it more important that the gospel be reasonable or that the gospel be hopeful? Arius's understanding was about as reasonable as any twentieth-century "baby boomer" could want—and about as impotent. Athanasius's understanding was about as hopeful as any twenty-first-century "Gen-Xer" could want—and about as irrational. The church sided with Athanasius—and a good thing it did, since Rome was about to burn.

The second group includes people like Benedict and the Celtic missionaries, but the biggest debate was probably between the disciples of Pelagius and the disciples of Augustine. The choice was (and is) this: Is it more important that an individual have the power to freely choose Christ, or that Christ have the power to freely choose the individual? Pelagius's understanding was every-thing the American educational/industrial elite could ever want. Augustine's understanding was everything marginal members of society could ever hope. The church sided with Augustine—and a good thing it did, since the Vikings were about to make every-body marginal.

E-mail #31
Subject: War of Words

Dear Christian Companion:

I'm sorry if I offended you by seemingly dismissing your favorite Reformation writers as part of a "low dogmatic period." Believe me, I am not saying that Luther or Calvin—or their later Anabaptist and Wesleyan companions—are shallow or unimportant. I am only saying that their world is less like our world than you think, and that their issues are less likely to be our issues today. The Reformation and the Counter-Reformation belong to a time when the abuses of Christendom needed to be corrected, but ours is a time when the excesses of paganism need to be defeated. Luther had to deal with feudal Christian kings and corrupt ecclesiastical princes. We have to deal (like Athanasius and Augustine before us) with Visigoths at the front door. It's hard to get too worked up about the credentialing of priests, the sale of indulgences, the proper organization of the parish, or even the authority of Scripture when barbarians are bombing the food court and a new "black plague" is devastating whole continents.

The key here is that we are in an age when the quest for politically correct ideology and dogmatically pure ideas is no longer important. This is a war of words that becomes a clash of creeds that all too easily becomes a blood feud. What we need is a new era of passionate dialogue . . . a sharing of hearts . . . a meeting of minds . . . a pursuit of truth.

Perhaps I can say it this way. We do not need to articulate the *truth* of Christianity, so much as to participate in the *trueing* of Christianity (a phrase I borrow from John Meagher's book *The Trueing of Christianity,* published by Doubleday in 1990). The experience of Jesus is being freshly elaborated as we speak.

E-mail #32
Subject: The Emerging Curriculum

Dear Christian Companion:

Attached to this e-mail is a brief summary of how I see the past curriculum of clergy education morphing into the present database that trains mission movers.

The Learning Content

Modern

- Bible
- Reformed-Modern History
- Systematic Theology
- World Religions
- Psychology of Religion
- Sociology of Religion
- Denominational Polity
- Counseling-Pastoral Care
- Clinical Pastoral Education (CPE)
- Theology and Public Policy
- Informational Worship

  to Glorify God
  Liturgy
  Expository preaching
  Hymnology

Postmodern

- Bible
- Patristic-Ancient History
- Christology
- Christian Missiology
- Holistic Health
- Cross-Cultural Sensitivity
- Team-based Organization
- Mentoring-Discipling
- Visioning

- Theology and Pagan Practice
- Experiential Worship

  to Motivate God's Mission
  Technology
  Motivational speaking
  Indigenous music

E-mail #33
Subject: The "Practical" Subjects

Dear Christian Companion:
I see you have a grasp of the shift in emphasis in the core subjects of theology, biblical studies, and history. Your confusion about the importance of "practical" subjects is understandable. You write: "But what about the practical subjects my denomina-

tion wants me to take in seminary? Are they even helpful anymore?"

When you approach the selection of "practical" subjects from a missiological (rather than ecclesiological) point of view, your expectations change. Get this: mission movers in the postmodern world are not called to *do* ministry, but to *motivate* and *equip* ministry. Once you understand this simple fact, your selection of "practical" subjects becomes both clearer and harder to accomplish. What is clear is that you want courses that *teach you how to equip others* in any given ministry, and not a course that teaches you how to do it by yourself. What is difficult is that most seminaries don't teach "practical" subjects this way, and because ministry is so contextual you have to look elsewhere in the mission field to find the training.

E-mail #34
Subject: The Hidden Assumption

Dear Christian Companion:
You misunderstand me. Practical ministry training is crucial—but it is more crucial that you are prepared to give it than that you receive it. Denominations and seminaries all want you to be practical. They want to equip you for excellence. The hidden assumption, however, is that *you* will be the primary practitioner. They teach on the assumption that *you* will be the primary preacher, sacramental celebrant, caregiver, counselor, administrator, organizer, etc. That assumption is valid for education for church leadership, but not for immersion in missional movement. For example, if I were teaching you to preach, I would not only teach you to communicate, but I would teach you to enforce a policy whereby you never preached unless at least two lay leaders had helped in the sermon preparation and literally stood with you before the congregation as you shared faith and hope. The object is for those lay leaders to preach, and to equip others to preach, who will equip others to preach, and so on and on. Seminary

trains you to do it alone, always and forever . . . and may God have mercy on your soul!

E-mail #35
Subject: What about Preaching?

Dear Christian Companion:
I can see why you want to talk about preaching! You write: "Yesterday my pastor introduced me to the denominational annual meeting among a small group of candidates for ordination. He announced with great pride that we aspired to be 'preachers,' and all the clergy in the room applauded wildly. Most of us just squirmed. Why am I so uncomfortable?"

You squirm because in your heart you know that preaching, as it has been traditionally experienced and taught, is a relative waste of time. And the last thing a true mission mover wants to do is spend hours each week wasting time. Sure, the relative value of preaching still varies from micro-culture to micro-culture, and is probably still more effective in Asian and African-American churches than Caucasian and Hispanic churches. Increasingly, however, it is merely an art form that is losing its audience, or merely a symbol of hierarchical authority that no longer influences life on the street.

Communication, persuasion, articulation, and expression all remain vitally important! It's just that the liturgical practice, preaching, and hymnology taught in seminaries and valued by denominations doesn't do it anymore. Professors may rail against it, organists may threaten union strikes, and institutional churches may fight over it, but you will be left wondering which God they are really trying to defend. It ain't yours! Your Jesus is learning how to use contemporary technologies, motivational medias, and indigenous music to reach each new micro-culture with the gospel. That's what you will have to learn, but you will probably learn more by skipping the seminary preaching and hymnology classes in order to hang around pop musicians, take a community college course in computer imaging, and get training in motivational speaking from Toastmasters.

E-mail #36
Subject: The Anger of the Established Church

Dear Christian Companion:
"I made the mistake of showing your latest e-mail to my pastor. Boy, was he mad! He said he was going to forward it to the bishop, and the bishop would probably cancel the next event EBA scheduled in our region. I hope I didn't get you into trouble."

Well, this sort of thing happens. I don't know your pastor, but from all the things you have said he seems like an essentially *faithful* Christian leader. Give him some time to think about it, and he may eventually come around. Modern seminaries teach pastors how God's Word is in fact a living "word," a creative experience that blows providentially through worship and all of life ... and then promptly tell them to forget about that and go write a sermon. But better yet, urge him to talk it over with his wife. Spouses always, always have a more realistic assessment of the relative power of preaching than do preachers.

I do know the bishop, and doubt that she will react the same way. The trend today is that most bishops are rediscovering what it means to be an apostolic leader from the New Testament, and are no longer trying to perpetuate a denominational heritage, make old strategies work again, or put old wine into new wineskins. If your pastor forwards my e-mail and a complaint to the bishop, she is more likely going to book a second EBA event *and* require your pastor to attend.

E-mail #37
Subject: Speaking of New Wine and Old Wineskins ...

Dear Christian Companion:
As long as we are talking about preaching, I might as well add that most of the training in worship design taught in seminaries

and celebrated in denominations falls far, far short of the needs of the mission field. I am not quite saying it is a waste of time . . . but almost. A basic intuition of worship as a reenactment of confession and forgiveness, learning and mission motivation, and lifestyle covenant is a very good thing. And if your bedrock beliefs include special appreciation for the sacraments, you would do well to ponder symbol and mystery. Much of the rest, however, is all accommodation to dated European cultural forms.

I have written about this elsewhere (e.g., in *Growing Spiritual Redwoods*), so I don't need to explain to you what "indigenous, experiential worship" is. The training to design such worship, however, is hard to find. I recommend apprenticeships in "out of the box" churches, and especially with congregational leaders of non-western cultures.

E-mail #38
Subject: How to Build a Nervous Breakdown
          into Your Career Path

Dear Christian Companion:
I'm glad you asked about the relevance of training in counseling, pastoral care, clinical pastoral education, psychology, and the like. By themselves, these are profound subjects, and if you are called to be a professional therapist or institutional chaplain (noble and vital callings!) you need to immerse yourself in them. Truth to tell, you are better off skipping seminary altogether, and taking an advanced degree in the university. The emerging pagan world will give you more respect and opportunity. A professional psychotherapist who is also a Christian can do wonderful, widely credible mission. A professional pastor who pretends to be a psychotherapist will get sued.

Nowhere is the hidden assumption in seminary training more apparent than here. The seminary assumes that *you* will be the primary practitioner. The denomination assumes that *you should be* the primary practitioner. Everyone assumes you will be going room-to-room, door-to-door, nursing home-to-nursing home, counselee-to-counselee, doing one-on-one caregiving. The assumption may have worked in the nineteenth century, but today it is a recipe for disaster. They might as well add a course on how to survive your inevitable nervous breakdown. Mission movers are not primary caregivers to the congregation; they are equippers who train others to care.

E-mail #39
Subject: How Can That Be?!

Dear Christian Companion:
You ask: "How can that be? How can that happen?" I was shocked by the question, but then I remembered that you have come to consider ministry having grown up in a traditional church. That is a considerable handicap.

The pastor may not be the primary caregiver to the congregation; she or he is a primary caregiver to the cell group of core leaders. This is a basic principle of cellular organization. A leader takes primary responsibility for the holistic care and feeding of the 3-12 people in his or her team. The pastor cares for leaders, who in turn care for leaders, who in turn care for leaders, and so on. You grew up in a traditionally organized church made up of task groups and committees. Caregiving by the chairperson for the committee was secondary at best, and no one expected the staff to really do it in any serious intentional way. If the committee member is in hospital, the last person they want to see visit is the chairperson of the committee. Send for the pastor! And if it's a multi-staff ministry, only the senior top dog will do!

But in a team-based or cell-based church, the pastor doesn't visit. She doesn't need to. She has equipped team leaders to do serious caregiving. And this is the training that needs to be given to pastors.

E-mail #40
Subject: Organization

Dear Christian Companion:

"I showed my pastor your latest e-mails. I just wanted to see how he would react. After he stopped laughing hysterically he said, 'Bandy must never have been much of a pastor. If I stopped preaching and visiting, this church would go downhill so fast it would make your head spin.' He wants me to stop writing you."

Well, I am glad you haven't stopped writing me. In fact, I have been a very "successful" pastor in three denominations and two countries for over two decades. But after a near-nervous breakdown and several crises of conscience, I decided it would be healthier for me to be faithful instead of successful. Your pastor had better look around. The median age of his church is rising, the worship attendance is dropping, an annual operating deficit is becoming a tradition, and the primary mission field that is his zip code is more diverse and spiritually hungry than ever before. His church is going downhill fast, and his only response is to preach better and visit more.

This is really just an organizational issue ... and focuses my criticism of denominational and seminary "practical" training for ministry. Obsessed by protecting antiquated denominational polity, they are way behind the learning curve for new organizational models. Almost every good business school or university (Harvard among others) offers training for entrepreneurs. Non-hierarchical, non-bureaucratic, team-based organizational models are proliferating in corporate, industrial, social service, nonprofit, health care, and every other sector imaginable—except the church. And seminaries refuse to teach it. Go figure!

E-mail #41
Subject: The Great Fear of Spiritual Entrepreneurship

Dear Christian Companion:
I know: "The denomination doesn't like mavericks."
This is where cultural diversity and the speed of change are wreaking havoc on the franchise mentality of denominations and the tenured curriculums of seminaries. The old expectations for practical ministry training all assumed that tactics could and should be transferable from one church franchise to another, and from one cultural context to another. Among postmodern people, that kind of thinking is both impractical and laughable.

Whatever you need to study will come out of the public's yearning for holistic health and your cross-cultural sensitivity. If you study sociology, it will have more to do with lifestyles and micro-cultures than demographics. If you study psychology, it will have more to do with wellness than illness. This marks a huge shift in experiential learning. In the old days, you spent all week on the seminary campus and spent weekend doing "fieldwork." Today you need to spend the weekend (at most) on campus, and spend all week "experiencing the mission field." In the old days experts lectured on how to do ministry, and then you tried to apply it. Today, you learn for yourself to apply it, and bring the experts up to speed when you see them on the weekend.

What you will hear is that denominations and seminaries fear "creeping congregationalism." Even congregationally based denominations fear it. It is the fear of independence, innovation, and yes, competition. The assumption is that there is more integrity in failing together than in a single maverick's success. "Education for church leadership" nurtures a standardized mediocrity that fears adaptation and values continuity. You seek to be immersed in a missional movement that values adaptability and fears corporate addiction. The best thing a seminary could teach a mission mover is how to learn from failure, how to find a way, and how to never give up until the micro-culture for whom your heart bursts experiences the transforming power of God and joins Jesus on the road to more mission.

The Critical Path

E-mail #42
Subject: Where's Jesus ... and How Can I Join Him?

Dear Christian Companion:
"Well, you have me more excited about ministry than ever before, and more confused about how to go about equipping myself to do it than ever before! Should I pursue ordination or not? Should I go to seminary or not? Can you paint a picture of how people like me can get on with Christ's mission with integrity?"

I confess that your question above has caused me considerable anxiety. It always scares me when somebody actually listens to me.

The central question (now and always) is this: *Where do you think Jesus will be fifteen years down the road to mission, and what do you need to learn in order to join him there?*

In the old days of education for church leadership, the call was a generic call to the ministries of word, sacrament, pastoral care, and service, and the training equipped a person to fulfill that generic call wherever he or she happened to get a job or be appointed by a bishop. "Have professional clergy toolkit, will travel" should have been written on every clergy business card.

Today in the era of the mission mover, the call is specific to a micro-culture and requires the acquisition of whatever skill is contextually relevant to help those people experience the transforming power of God and become disciples of Jesus. The training, therefore, must likewise be just as contextual. "Have passionate love for you in particular, will do whatever it takes" should be written on every mission mover's business card.

So long as the denomination keeps thinking in terms of a generic call, the seminary will keep training generic church leaders. So long as the seminary keeps training generic church leaders, the seminary will keep deploying them to pursue a generic call.

E-mail #43
Subject: Are Ordination and Seminary Worthless?

Dear Christian Companion:

Remember: I did not say that ordination and seminary training were worthless. I said that the denomination and the seminary were no longer the dominant players in education for mission immersion. They may play a part ... but it is a secondary and supportive role. For example, if the priestly celebrations of the sacraments are crucial to your bedrock beliefs, then you may want to seek ordination. If your heart is bursting to help middle-class, traditionally educated, professional micro-cultures, then you might want an academic degree in theology.

Now what would happen if the denomination stopped defining ordination as a generic call? Their own seminaries would become irrelevant. What would happen if the seminary stopped providing generic training? The denomination would become irrelevant to their graduates. In a sense, this is already happening in both ways, and the gap between seminary and denomination is widening. There are judicatories and seminaries that are beginning to awaken to the real challenges of the pagan world, and that are starting to nurture and train mission movers for more than church leadership.

E-mail #44
Subject: But How Do I Do It?!

Dear Christian Companion:

Fair enough! Let me outline the critical path through which education for mission immersion is happening. This is the path through which mission movers are emerging as the leaders of the postmodern church. This path may happen intentionally, unintentionally, or, most commonly, as a combination of planning and providence.

✓ Discover your "heartburst." The single most important thing to begin the journey is for you to isolate the
connection between call and culture that thrills, challenges, and motivates you to the core of your being. It's
not a call to the world, or the church, or the ministry. It
is a call to a particular micro-culture … a specific lifestyle
group … an identifiable group of people.

✓ Find a mentor. Form an ongoing relationship with a
mentor who shares your core values and bedrock beliefs,
empathizes with your call, and can help network you
with learning experiences and coaching partners. This
person needs to be available to you face-to-face, but also
through 24-hour long-distance communication.

✓ Join a cohort. Unite with a team, or a companionship
of travelers, much like Paul traveled with Silas, Luke,
Priscilla, Lydia, Timothy, and Onesimus. Separately or
together, wherever you go, whatever you do, this is your
primary support group for prayer, critique, planning, and
support.

✓ Assemble learning modules. Stop thinking in terms
of curriculum, faculty, or campus, and plan your learning
path one module at a time. You may take a course in Bible
from a seminary in the Northeast, then skip to a history
class from a university in the Midwest, and then join an
online forum in cross-cultural ministry from an
Australian pastor half the world away. A module is any
pragmatically useful package of learning that will help
you leverage the mission for which your heart bursts.

✓ Become a pilgrim. Design half a dozen six-to-twelve-
week placements in actual ministries, anywhere in the
world, that are contextually relevant to your mission. Live
with them. Apprentice yourself to their leaders. Push the
limits of your comfort, and test your creativity.

✓ Cross any disciplinary boundaries. Seek training one
class or one experience at a time in business, law, media,
communications, organizational management, interper-
sonal relationships, or any other discipline that emerges

as relevant from your pilgrimage. It doesn't matter where. Find the best person, the best place, the best class, or the best opportunity and do it.

✓   Network constantly. Use the Internet to learn, network, and communicate with your mentor and cohort. Read and collect e-books, not hard copy. Track hyperlinks, not bibliographies. Synthesize media, and do not limit yourself to reading. Train yourself to access forums at the airport or the media café, and to communicate instantly on the subway or in a wilderness.

✓   Fail boldly. You will constantly make mistakes, so develop a plan to learn from them. It is better to take a wrong turn in the passionate pursuit of a holy destination than to linger too long over a strategic plan to avoid damaging your career. The people who learn the most are unafraid of humiliation. The leaders who accomplish the most know what it means to be a "fool for Christ."

Think of it this way. Education for church leadership is like a fixed-price menu in the denominational restaurant. You pay for the whole thing at once, eat what you are served from appetizer through dessert, and if you complain to the chef he will condescendingly suggest you must not be a gourmet. Education for mission immersion is like eating a la carte. You pay as you go, eat what you choose, and if the food doesn't satisfy you, fire the chef.

E-mail #45
Subject: Fire the Chef?

Dear Christian Companion:
"Frankly, the critical path of learning seems pretty egocentric. You say, 'Eat what you like and fire the chef'! What if the foods I like are bad for me, and the chef really is a good nutritionist?"

When we first started talking I spoke of the need for a vital relationship with a mentor. There is no reason why a professor, tutor, guidance counselor, supervising minister or other faculty members and institutional officers cannot be mentors ... but the fact is, this is all too rare. True mentors risk real relationship. And real relationship dares to be mutually critical, constantly conversational, and deeply respectful of the spiritual depth that lies in both student and teacher.

The problem with the "chef" in my metaphor is not the profession but the condescension. It is the condescension that a fixed-price menu or a standardized core curriculum is the best plan for every micro-culture on earth. It is the condescension that an "expert" can dictate the diet that is best for your personal metabolism. It is the condescension that a professional should define "good food" with indifference to your state of mind, place in life, and the mysterious working of the Spirit in your heart. It is the condescension that any "chef" can also determine the "dining experience" that must necessarily be most profound and most relevant in your life and mission. That's the problem. It's the inherent, unrecognized condescension that is the problem. And the more our world resembles the ancient world, the more that irritant rubs us raw.

You can find a different kind of chef ... if you prayerfully look. You want a chef who is willing to be in relationship. You need a chef who will select food, cook food, and present food customized for your life, your mission, and the unique work of the Spirit in your heart. They know how to serve a la carte. Occasionally, they will insist that you try an unpleasant dish, served in an aesthetically displeasing way, but it is not for the sake of their standards. It is for the sake of your unique mission.

Remember that Jesus did not prescribe a diet or determine a dining experience. He provided a banquet and allowed people to select the food, eat the food, or distribute the food in any way that would accomplish the Great Commission.

E-mail #46
Subject: The Pilgrim Band

Dear Christian Companion:

As I prayed for you last night, and reflected our recent correspondence, it suddenly occurred to me that when you responded
to the metaphor about the chef and the banquet you were assum-
ing that you were *dining alone*.

That is the assumption most traditional education makes. Sure,
you bond with your classmates and share study groups, but fundamentally education for church leadership "serves" you as an
individual because they assume your denomination will deploy
you as an individual. That assumption is no longer valid. Instead,
you dine with *friends*. You eat, drink, travel, minister, and lead as
a companionship.

A "companionship" is a mutually mentoring cell group of co-
workers whose mission is compatible with your calling. Such a
companionship can be formal or informal, contractual or volunteer. You may find yourself in the role of apprentice to master, or
student to teacher, or disciple to apostle, or explorer to native
guide, or trainee to executive, or player to coach, or any number
of combinations. Education for mission immersion is composed
of overlapping, abiding, influential relationships that do not com-
partmentalize the acquisition and application of knowledge, but
that blend the two together seamlessly in the context of your
lifestyle.

E-mail #47
Subject: The Right Companions

Dear Christian Companion:

"But Tom, my denomination and at least one seminary I am
talking with do understand about relationships, too. The denomination will sponsor a breakfast once a quarter for the candidates,
and the seminary organizes study groups in the dormitory. Isn't
that great!"

Oh well . . . I see that I must explain myself further. When Paul and Barnabas handpicked their missionary companions, they did not offer a core curriculum, study groups in the library, guidance counseling for "field education," and quarterly breakfasts with the denominational executive. Education for mission immersion is taking us back before John Dewey and the standardization of university training, all the way back to ancient methods of tutoring disciples.

In modern times, relationships have been an incidental extra benefit that occasionally enhanced the abstract learning process. In ancient/contemporary times, relationships are the necessary matrix in which personal growth happens. And those relationships do not "stand outside" our lifestyle, so that in order to become educated we must "leave behind" normal life to fulfill course requirements or attend meetings. Those relationships unfold in both strategic and chaotic fashion in the very midst of our lifestyle. They cross over between disciplines.

E-mail #48
Subject: Boundary Crossing

Dear Christian Companion:
A second key element in this emerging critical path is intentional boundary crossing. Education for church leadership assumes that you can essentially remain on one campus, in a single degree program, and among limited institutional learning environments. Sure, you can study a year abroad or do an interim year of fieldwork, but essentially you connect with one location. And sure, you can choose among electives in the degree program and even take a course or two in another university, but essentially you relate to a single registrar. And yes, you can do clinical work in a hospital or correctional center, but these are limited to counseling and pastoral care. You will have no opportunity to learn how to be Christian in a small business, corporate, government, nonprofit or other discipline.

The critical path of the future intentionally crosses geographic, cultural, and disciplinary boundaries. And not just as a temporary blip in the curriculum, but as a real and complete leap in the personal growth journey. The anchor in the chaos of boundary crossing is not residency, or curriculum, or compatible career paths. The anchor is the pilgrim band, the drive for contextual relevance, and the passion to be with Jesus on the road to mission.

As in earliest church times, Christianity will thrive in the future through lifestyle models and mentoring relationships networking through business, social service, nonprofit and other public sectors ... not through parish churches. So you need to cross those boundaries in order to prepare for the emerging mission tactics. I met a former denominational executive who resigned to train as a pastry chef ... and claims she is having more mission impact and growing deeper Christian community in her shop than she ever did in her denomination.

E-mail #49
Subject: Learning from Failure

Dear Christian Companion:

I thought my allusion to the mission-driven pastry chef might interest you! I see it has simultaneously raised excitement and stress. You ask: "If I don't know what tactic will work best, how do I seek the training I will need?"

That's the rub. You don't know what will work best. The one thing you do know is that the traditional "parish church tactic" that you are being trained to do is probably not it (or at least not all of it). Even if you cross boundaries to learn a variety of tactics, you may not know what the best tactic will be. You may arrive amid the micro-culture for whom your heart bursts, and the "how" may still elude you.

That's why the best thing a seminary could teach is simply the process to learn from your inevitable mistakes. You *will* fail. That's a given. The question is: Can you pick yourself up from the dust and ridicule, evaluate, learn, and try again until you reach the micro-culture for whom your heart bursts? The abilities for self-analysis and mission synthesis are crucial. And the need for high self-esteem is essential.

E-mail #50
Subject: How the Heck Am I Going to Pay for This?

Dear Christian Companion:
"The critical path raises an important question for me. How the heck am I going to pay for this? I can foresee there are enrollment costs, travel costs, food and accommodation costs, technology costs, and who knows what else. I may want to train in modules, but seminaries and universities want me to sign up for the degree program."

The truth is that whether you do education for church leadership, or education for mission immersion, you probably can't afford it. It would be nice if denominational subsidies, seminary bursaries, or even Lilly Foundation grants could be shifted to support education for mission immersion. Maybe it will happen in some places, because this reallocation of funds would be in the best interest of the Christian movement in North America. But probably it will not happen, because most denominations and seminaries are more interested in institutional survival.

Here is your choice. You can go into financial debt to be educated for church leadership, pay most of the expense up front, and then carry the debt after you have burned out, dropped out, or opted out of the church leadership for which you paid so much to be trained. Or, you can pay as you go, manage your debt piece-meal, and be educated for mission immersion that may never make you rich but will certainly fulfill your life. You may have to do what Paul did—stop for a while in Ephesus to make tents before buying that ticket to Corinth.

E-mail #51
Subject: There Is No Career Path

Dear Christian Companion:

"My husband has a question. He asks: 'When will it end? When will you graduate? When will your career effectively begin?' He has a job, too. He wants to raise a family. And while he is a Christian, and supports my call to ministry, he wants to have some predictability and stability in our lives. What will I tell him?"

It will never end. You will never graduate. You have already begun. There is no career path—only a spiritual life. There is no safety net—only entrepreneurship. I suspect that Priscilla and Aquila either traveled together, or negotiated their family planning around their mission. I know that is hard, and it may not be what your family ever anticipated doing, but there is really no way around it. The combination of the emerging pagan world, and the tramp of Jesus beyond Emmaus, allows fewer alternatives. Denominational pension plans are under stress; there are fewer and fewer traditional congregations that can afford salaried personnel; and the mission field keeps moving faster and faster.

In my dictionary, the words "careen" and "career" follow one after the other. Your husband wants you to have a career. He wants you to "advance through life, progress through the history of an institution, and pursue a profession." Tell him that is no longer possible in the contemporary/ancient world. It wasn't possible for Paul, Silas, Lydia, Priscilla, and Aquila. It is not possible for you.

Instead, you are going to "careen." You are going to "rush head-long, hurtle unsteadily, tilt, lean over, knock things down, and cause things to happen."

"Careening" down the road to mission is not what most spouses signed up for in their marriage vows. He wants you to "career" down the road to financial security, family stability, predictable holidays, and healthy retirement. There is nothing wrong with this. Even the apostles wanted this. The difference is that they wanted to be with Jesus *more*.

4

HOW WILL YOU ENDURE IT TO THE END?

E-mail #1
Subject: The Hard Part

Dear Christian Pilgrim:

Given our past correspondence, it may sound odd to say that we really haven't talked about the "hard part" yet. The deep prayer and reflection and wrestling with illusions and self-doubts, the struggle to focus contextually relevant content and methods of learning and pay the price to do it (financial and existential)—this was all the "easy" part! Now you have to surrender your lifestyle on a daily basis to one of the most unpopular career paths in contemporary North American culture.

Paul complained (2 Corinthians 11:21-29) of *his* labors. He listed the imprisonments, floggings, lashings, beatings, stonings, and shipwrecks. He enumerated the dangers of travel, bandits, and foreign micro-cultures. And he remembered the sleepless nights, hunger, and cold. He worried constantly about his traveling companions and the many people he had convinced to do the crazy, risky thing of believing in Christ. The point is not that you will experience these hardships, but simply that representing Christ in the pagan world isn't easy.

E-mail #2
Subject: Where's Jesus ... and How Can I Keep Up?

Dear Christian Pilgrim:
"My God, I want to be with Jesus! More than anything else! What keeps me awake at night is that in the midst of my human-ness and weakness and addictedness, I might lose sight of Jesus along the way."

Earlier I said that the central question is this: *Where do you think Jesus will be fifteen years down the road to mission—and what are you willing to stake in order to join him there?* The same central question will dog your footsteps all along the journey: *Where is Jesus going ... and what am I willing to stake to keep up with him along the way?*

What micro-culture will Jesus be among, what transforma-tional purpose will he be about, what challenge will he be addressing? And what price will you be willing to pay to change your assumptions, adapt your lifestyle, acquire different skills, and invest your personal and financial stability in order to join Jesus there? This is more than personal strategic planning. This is desire to be with Jesus. As Paul said: "I have suffered the loss of all things, and I regard them as rubbish, in order that I may gain Christ.... I want to know Christ and the power of his resurrec-tion and the sharing of his sufferings" (Phil. 3:8, 10).

E-mail #3
Subject: Staking It All

Dear Christian Pilgrim:
Your ability to endure is directly connected with your desire to go. The most telling story of the mission to the gentiles is the one about Philip's encounter on the Gaza Road with the Ethiopian. It

begins with the words: "Then an angel of the Lord said to Philip, 'Get up and go. . . .' So he got up and went" (Acts 8:26-27). It's as simple as that. This is the biblical meaning of "humility" recovered in the monastic movement and emerging once again as the single most important quality of the mission mover. Those who are educated for mere church leadership do not endure because deep in their hearts they never really wanted to go. They wanted people to come. They wanted to shape the mission around their lifestyle, protect their comfort zones, provide security for their families, and so on. When those safety nets become threatened, or those comfort zones become breached (and, rest assured, culture will threaten the former and the Holy Spirit will breach the latter), then they lose momentum, change career paths, or despair.

"Enduring" is hard. Indeed, it is not a rational act. The rational thing to do is to run away, cease and desist, accommodate, compromise, find an alternative path. And indeed, a good mission mover will do all of that as well. They are not stupid, nor are they willfully masochistic. It's just that there are times (more times than you think) when neither culture nor the Holy Spirit will give you rational choices. Then you must make non-rational choices. You must endure.

Church leaders count the cost of discipleship because they imagine the ultimate godly choice will be to live or die for Christ. It isn't. Dying for Christ is the easy thing to do. The hardest choice is to endure for Christ. When Paul is faced with death, the easy choice is to die for Christ and live forever with the Lord (Phil. 1:21). His preference, however, is to keep on living for Christ and this is the harder alternative. Why would he do this? So that he can eventually grow a megachurch? Collect a good pension? Rise in the denominational ranks? Glean prestige from the community? Glory in a heritage protected? No. He makes the non-rational choice to simply "keep going" because that's where Jesus is and he wants to merge with Jesus. This is not a fellowship choice (*phileo*), nor is it a sacrificial choice (*agape*), but it is a passion choice (*eros*). You endure because you want to be where Jesus is.

E-mail #4
Subject: Can You Do It?

Dear Christian Pilgrim:
Your recent e-mail is one of the wisest, most self-aware messages you have sent me. I have never seen you so honest with yourself about your dreams and shortcomings. "Can I do this—*really?*" Would that every prospective seminarian would ask such a question!

Here is the measuring stick of faithfulness. Count the cost of discipleship in each category, and in this order:

- Attitude costs—changes to your worldview
- Heritage costs—changes to your world
- Lifestyle costs—changes to your daily behavior
- Leadership costs—changes to your learning curve
- Organizational costs—changes to your partnerships
- Property costs—changes to what you own
- Financial costs—changes to what you prioritize

Count the cost of discipleship in these categories, in this order, and on a regular basis. You will use the same chart with the official board of any congregation with whom you are walking with Jesus. This is the discipleship of pilgrim bands on the road to mission.

If you are willing to pay the price in the top categories, then paying the price in changing what you own and changing what you prioritize will not be as hard as you think. If you are willing to pay the price, then I guarantee—actually, not I, but the Holy Spirit guarantees—that you WILL endure.

E-mail #5
Subject: What about Ordination?

Dear Christian Pilgrim:
Yes, all this does seem to make ordination relatively trivial. It is a bit presumptuous of an ecclesiastical institution to put itself in the place of God to certify anybody for Christian mission. It made

a little more sense in the nineteenth century, when ordination shifted from empowerment in the Holy Spirit to recognition of professional skills, because at least the skills that were being recognized had in themselves an "enduring character." But now that the skills you learn today become obsolete overnight, even that shift in ordination is meaningless.

What we are really talking about, however, is the recovery of the real essence of ordination. Ordination celebrates among your Christian pilgrim band the desire to go that will, in turn, allow you to endure. That's all it really is, and all it needs to be, and all that it should be. Making it a matter of heritage preservation, or polity obedience, or job guarantee, or participation in a health care plan not only sidetracks the meaning of ordination, but gets in the way of the power of ordination. The very fact that ordination has come to mean these *other* things ensures that in a pagan world the one ordained will not, and cannot, endure to the end.

E-mail #6
Subject: Spare Me

Dear Christian Pilgrim:

Oh please spare me the pomposity about being "a chosen race, a royal priesthood, a holy nation, God's own people. . .proclaim[ing] the mighty acts of him who called you out of darkness into his marvelous light" (1 Peter 2:9)! James's circle was always trying to measure itself against the standard of the Jerusalem Temple. Their visions of greatness may have been theologically sound, but when applied to practical ministry are tinged with smugness and sound more like delusions of grandeur. No wonder the Jerusalem church hauled Paul and Barnabas back to the head office in Acts 15. Here James and his cronies were posturing as a royal priesthood, while Paul was scrambling across the countryside consorting with runaway slaves, women, and retailers.

Your theologically correct quote is the kind of thing church leaders say when they are safe in Christendom, and the biggest threats to mission are poor standards of percentage giving and a disrespectful mayor. The "Jerusalem Church" uses the quote at ordination ceremonies and whenever clergy get together to belly-ache about life. "I work too hard, I don't get paid enough, my parishioners are petty, and the funeral home stiffed me on the fee this week, but thank God I belong to the 'royal priesthood'!"

E-mail #7
Subject: I Apologize . . . Sort Of

Dear Christian Pilgrim:
I felt badly as soon as I hit "send" in the last e-mail, and you are right to chastise me for being overly bitter. Then again, I've been in "the ministry" for thirty years and have a few things to be bitter about. Even Paul said it was "madness" for him to speak like this, but he complained anyway. That's what I mean about endurance: to feel the bitterness, complain and lament, and then still keep doing what you are doing.

I think what hurt Paul most is revealed in his allusion to "danger from my own people" (2 Corinthians 11:26). Given the context of the verse, he was probably thinking of the rejection of his own Jewish Pharisaic comrades. Yet it is also clear that his own Christian "brothers and sisters" more than once undermined, sabotaged, and obstructed his work and abused his reputation. The "royal priesthood" turned out not to be a very "loyal priesthood." Today many factions have shattered the solidarity and trusted mutual support of the denominations into which many clergy were ordained, and clergy are victimized from within the church as much as from beyond the church.

E-mail #8
Subject: How Do We Dare to Use the Royal "We"?

Dear Christian Pilgrim:
You write: "Whatever the sins of the institutional church in the world, we are still part of an invisible, eternal, universal church

that is the bride of Christ. This 'holy nation' or 'chosen people' presents a standard of 'priesthood' to which I should aspire . . . right?"

In the latter years of Christendom, clergy liked to frame their self-evaluation in this contrast between the "visible" and "invisible" church. It was an ecclesiastical attempt to interpret (and perhaps excuse) the imperfections of the institutional church. Yet in pre-Christendom and post-Christendom times (i.e., the time of Paul and the time today), such ecclesiastical attempts to frame self-evaluation are irrelevant. Paul's frame of reference was purely missiological. It had nothing to do with interpreting imperfections within an institution, since no church institutions existed. Only the mission movement to share the experience of Jesus existed.

The context of self-evaluation today, therefore, is not in the contrast between the "visible" and "invisible" church, but between "the body of Christ *in residence*" and "the body of Christ *in motion*." I wrote about this contrast in my previous books *Roadrunner* and *Fragile Hope*. Here is the point for our conversation:

The body of Christ *in residence* (that's the institutional propertied church that spends 80 percent of its budget protecting sacred space, sacred people, and sacred time) quotes 1 Peter 2:9 and applies it to the clergy. *The clergy* are the royal priesthood, *the denomination* is the holy nation, and *the congregational members who contribute to the stewardship campaign* are the chosen people.

The body of Christ *in motion*, however (that's the traveling companionship of apostles trying to "become all things to all people, that [they might] by all means save some" described in 1 Cor. 9:22), quotes 1 Peter 2:9 and applies it to Christian disciples. *The community* is the royal priesthood, *the missional movement* is the migratory holy nation, and *the seekers, newcomers, and other God-fearers whose attention has been captured by Jesus* are the chosen people.

Once you have made that distinction, NOW ask yourself how you will endure being a minister to the very end. It means your primary support group is not a judicatory but a band of pilgrims, your loyalty is not to a denomination but to a mission, and your accountability does not lie in the boardroom of the church but the food court of the shopping mall.

And once you have drawn that conclusion, NOW ask why the seminary that trained you, the denomination that certified you, and the congregation that hired you are now all madder than blazes at you.

E-mail #9
Subject: A Tale of Two Processes

Dear Christian Pilgrim:

Yes, I thought my last post would give you pause for thought! You are quite correct in observing that the traditional seminary will train you for the body of Christ in residence, and the denomination will deploy you among bodies of Christ in residence, and those franchised bodies of Christ in residence will fully expect you to *stay in residence!* Keep office hours, maintain fixed worship times, renovate the property slowly and with great concern for memorial plaques, and above all, keep the other residents happy!

The stress you will endure is a kind of continuation of the stress you experienced when you first tried to explain your original call to the church officials, and when you first tried to customize your course load and learning path with the guidance counselor of a prospective seminary. It just gets worse now.

Forget the mission statement and the welcoming rhetoric on the church sign on the front lawn. The core process of the body of Christ in residence is to attract people in, sort out the people who most look like us, inform them with what we think they need to know, slot them into management, and raise their standard of stewardship. In return, they will be privileged to enjoy worship in their own aesthetic tastes, free stuff like weddings and funerals, and the personal and immediate attention of the pastor.

Unfortunately, your call from the beginning has been to immerse yourself in mission as a passionate apostle rather than head an ecclesiastical institution as a trained professional. Can you spell S-T-R-E-S-S?

The core process that interests you is one in which seekers are transformed by the experience of Christ, grow into the likeness of Christ, and are drawn to fulfill their destinies by walking with Christ in mission. All you can promise in return is that they will enjoy a profound camaraderie with their fellow pilgrims, they will feel terrific, and they will have you as a mentor and guide.

So one of things you will have to endure as a minister is that you are essentially unemployable among a substantial number of institutional churches in North America today, and that your seminary alumni connections and denominational personnel processes are not highly motivated to place you.

E-mail #10
Subject: Of Course It's Not Hopeless

Dear Christian Pilgrim:

I did not mean to scare you, and the future is certainly *not* hopeless. There are "bodies of Christ *in motion*" out there who are looking for leaders like yourself. And even within traditional Christendom churches, there are more and more restless, faithful church people who want to leave residence *to become* the body of Christ in motion. And if you look to growing immigrant groups or among people whose origins are not indigenous to North America, or if you look to emerging generations of people young of heart or young of body with deep spirituality, you will find still others eager for your leadership. And even among established seminaries and denominational judicatories, there are a few who will train and deploy a mission mover like you.

I am not saying it is impossible. I am only recognizing that it will be challenging.

E-mail #11
Subject: The Biggest Challenge to Your Perseverance

Dear Christian Pilgrim:

The fundamental reason church leaders burn out, drop out, or opt out is that they are ultimately destroyed by the co-dependency fostered by the body of Christ *in residence*. The symptoms might involve irreconcilable conflicts, theological disagreements, ideological perspectives, or even sexual misconduct. The results might be disability, radical career changes to nonreligious institutions, or shifts from parish ministry to institutional chaplaincy or judicatory roles or other faith-based nonprofits. In other words, the same underlying issue that causes potential ministry candidates to second-guess themselves and wonder why anyone would subject themselves to traditional parish leadership also causes veteran clergy to become used up by and fed up with their calling.

That cause is co-dependency. Co-dependency is an unhealthy relationship between needy people and a leader who has a need to be needed. It is not that the leader is merciful, but that the leader *has an obsessive need* to be merciful. It is not that the church people are in need, but that *they have an unhealthy desire for someone to take care of them.* That's co-dependency. And the unpleasant truth is that the body of Christ *in residence* fosters that co-dependency.

The more unpleasant truth is that the longer the body of Christ remains *in residence*, the more it magnetically attracts dysfunctional people into membership and leadership who have an obsessive need to tell people what to do or to be told what to do. The unwitting, co-dependent pastor welcomes these people because newcomers have slowed to a trickle and these dysfunctional people are willing to hold office and use offering envelopes. Yet needy pastor and needy people feed off each other, and ultimately love each other to death.

E-mail #12
Subject: A Terrible Way to Die

Dear Christian Pilgrim:

I don't blame you for weeping when you read my last message. I weep often. It is a terrible way for a pastor or a congregation to die, and yet we see it over and over again. Co-dependent relationships close in upon themselves and become ever more exclusive of others. Dysfunctional people shape the church around their personal tastes, political preferences, and family needs; and the pastor finds himself or herself spending more and more energy on fewer and fewer families, always taking care of the membership and rarely interacting with the wider public that is the real mission target of Christ. I sometimes call these dysfunctional people "controllers." It's not just that they want to tell the pastor what to do. They want the pastor to shape her or his ministry around their expectations. Two things result:

- What once was a trickle of newcomers now ceases altogether. The median age of the congregation rises. The core leaders chronically complain about "doing everything" and yet never let go of it.
- Revolutions rock the church, as factions vie for the control to shape the program around *their* tastes, perspectives, and needs, and the power to control the pastoral agenda.

Eventually the co-dependent pastor burns out from trying to preserve harmony and keep everybody happy, or drops out to take a more lucrative and peaceful job in another career that will revive the failing health of his or her marriage and family, or opts out to take a "call" to another church or position in the religious institution.

Unfortunately, they carry the same co-dependency with them to the next church, and the cycle simple repeats itself. The few survivors of this cycle of despair become adept at conflict management, denominational personnel policy, parliamentary procedure, and "conning" the congregation with their ingratiating and friendly ways. Yet they are dying inside, and the church is dying around them, and the mission is dying beyond them. And for what? To care for a decreasing number of needy people in order to fulfill the rapacious need to be needed.

E-mail #13
Subject: Separating "Needy People" from "People in Need"

Dear Christian Pilgrim:

I rather expected you would ask this question, because a lot of church leaders get mad at me when I identify this co-dependency that is destroying them, their church, and God's mission. People get most angry about the things they chronically deny. You write: "But Tom! Isn't the church supposed to reach out and include the poor, the broken, the hungry and thirsty, the trapped and abused, and the victims of this world? Isn't that what pastors are supposed to facilitate?"

You need to distinguish between people with authentic need, and "needy" people. The two groups are not the same, although there certainly are people who are *both* in genuine need *and* obsessive about manipulating others to take care of them in their need. Usually, however, people in genuine need resent others trying to take care of them, just as genuinely healthy leaders resent being sucked into dependent relationships.

"Needy people" whine about problems, prioritize their agendas above all others, obsess over relative trivialities, and invest more time and energy trying to control authorities, policies, and procedures to bend to their wishes than in solving their own problems. They do anything to protect their membership privileges, and never really listen to the concerns of outsiders. They are like alcoholics who argue vehemently about trivialities, avoid the real issues, and stalk out of the room when they do not get their way.

"People in need" feel urgent about their problems, but are not insensitive to the fact that other people have their own problems. "People in need" are also people who know how to give, offer support to others, and demonstrate kindness beyond themselves. They have no compulsion to control the organization that helps them, and are apt to support the organization in helping others once their problems have been addressed.

"Needy people" are often remarkably rich in goods and opportunities, but incredibly stingy in giving to others. "People in need" are often remarkably poor in goods and opportunities, but incredibly generous in giving what little they possess to others. I think the best contrast is to say that "people in need" have a life beyond their need, but "needy people" make their need their life.

But note this: The very fact that you have trouble distinguishing between needy people and people in genuine need reveals that you carry within you this temptation to co-dependency. Just as the predilection to alcoholism can be inherited, so also this temptation to co-dependency has been ingrained in you through a lifetime of growing up in Christendom.

E-mail #14
Subject: Marriage Metaphors

Dear Christian Pilgrim:
Although I have avoided using marriage as a metaphor, I can see why your reflections since our last correspondence have been on this theme. Co-dependency is often associated with unhealthy marriages. However, I caution against using marriage as a metaphor to describe the relationship between pastor and congregation.

You follow a common Christendom practice when you say that the pastor should care for the church in the same way as a husband or wife should care for his or her spouse. Certainly there are similarities in the way both relationships are typified by mutual sensitivity, cooperation to attain shared goals, and the birthing of new disciples. Nevertheless, the marriage metaphor applied to the pastoral relationship is not biblical . . . and with good reason.

The biblical marriage metaphor describes the church as the bride *of* Christ. It is dangerous to allow the pastor to usurp the role of Christ in the marriage metaphor. If you think this way as a pastor of a congregation, your stress level will grow and your ability to endure the challenges of ministry will lessen. Your inevitable quarrels with the church will be much harder to resolve. You will trap yourself into unnecessary dilemmas between "my wife the church" and "my wife," and between "my mission as an apostle" and "my duty to my church family." These dilemmas induce enormous and debilitating guilt, and they are unnecessary.

The church is *not* your spouse. Therefore, you are free to be more visionary and prophetic, and free to pursue your mission with and beyond the church. If you must think in family metaphors, think of yourself as the eldest and most mature child helping to raise the siblings to leave home as mature Christians.

E-mail #15
Subject: Family Metaphors

Dear Christian Pilgrim:
I have mixed emotions when you write glorifying your personal church experience as "a great church family." Family systems theory is often used by the "body of Christ *in residence*" to justify its obsession with harmony and its refusal to grow. What they mean by "family" and "family ministry" is the desire to nurture their own members or maximize mutual support among their members. Therefore, certain programs figure prominently in their strategic plans:

- Children's Christian education
- Families worshiping together
- Church anniversaries and homecomings
- Seniority of long-standing members

The bottom line for the "family" church is that it will always, always be more important to keep people than to welcome people. New people are welcome, but only insofar as they do not alienate people already there. The creative, missional edge is always dulled. Over time, adult spiritual discipline weakens; the family unit worshiping together gives way to empty-nesters and then aging widows sitting together; church anniversaries become nostalgic hotbeds of discontent and longing for the good old days; and repeated attempts at long-range planning repeatedly fade away.

The problem with the family metaphor is that the basic goal *to get the kids out of the house* is always ignored. The point of the family is to grow children into maturity, so that they will *leave home* and grow another family. But "family churches" never grow other "families"! They just keep to themselves. The mark of a true "family" is not that they love each other and want to come home, but that they love each other enough to kick the kids out of the nest to start another nest.

A big reason clergy burn out, drop out, or opt out is simply that they grow utterly bored and frustrated working with the same people all the time. In a human family, the family members who misbehave get a disproportionate amount of attention, and in a church family, the members who act out of bounds get a disproportionate amount of attention from the pastor and official board. Five years in a family church, and pastors spend most of their time with about six dysfunctional families endlessly repeating the same bad habits and ineffective interventions.

E-mail #16
Subject: The Ancient Fight between the Body of Christ
in Residence and the Body of Christ in Motion

Dear Christian Pilgrim:
I first wrote about this in *Roadrunner* and *Fragile Hope*. You have to understand that the first nine chapters of the Acts of the Apostles describe a *failed* strategic plan. The first attempt of the earliest church to follow the Great Commission was to stay put, own property, invite all the micro-cultures to come to them to experience the gospel, and teach newcomers to adapt themselves to the religious institutions of their time. When the Bible says they tried to have a community that held "all things in common," it

means more than sharing the basic necessities of life. This failed strategic plan tried to impose a unified budget, a uniformity of institutional behavior, and a blended worship experience that would please everyone all at once. Sound familiar? The body of Christ in residence spends 80 percent of its budget and energy protecting sacred space, sacred people, and sacred time, holds great potluck suppers, maximizes harmony, and celebrates blended contemporary worship.

It took the Holy Spirit about eight or ten chapters in Acts to kick the disciples out of Jerusalem to become the body of Christ *in motion*. This was the mission to the gentiles. The body of Christ in motion is always on the road, constantly adapting, innovating, and changing, so that by every means possible it can help as many people as possible experience Jesus and walk in his way. The stories about Philip on the Gaza Road, Paul on the Damascus Road, and Peter on the road between Joppa and Caesarea all illustrate the stressful shift away from a failed strategic plan. We are experiencing the same stress today as we leave Christendom behind.

E-mail #17
Subject: The Lure of the Head Office in Jerusalem

Dear Christian Pilgrim:
"I asked my pastor to tell me his story of life in the ministry. He told me all about the fun and friends in seminary, the struggling little rural church that was his first parish, the move to a program church, his personnel work in the middle judicatory, and his aspirations for community influence and denominational significance. I guess he has fully recovered from his recent heart attack."

The reason there is such tension between the body of Christ in residence and the body of Christ in motion is that the lure of "Jerusalem" is so insidious. It would be one thing if the stress between the two modes of the body of Christ were simply a matter of conflict and confrontation. The head office in Jerusalem summoned Paul and Silas to accountability in Acts 15. Bang! There was a big argument about whether new Christians needed to be circumcised, taught to eat the right food groups and appreciate the right music, trained to use church envelopes, and swear allegiance to the denominational polity. Unfortunately, outright conflict is only the tip of the iceberg. Most of the stress is hidden, ready to rip the hull and heart of the most competent pastor.

Christendom clergy were ordained to a place or a program (to this parish or that parish; with tasks to preach and sacraments to distribute, or as counsel, advocate, etc.). Inevitably this translates into a "call to career." The same congregational co-dependency between needy people and clergy who need to be needed is reenacted in the denomination. Needy clergy become co-dependent with a denomination that needs to be needed. Success is measured by the climb up the career ladder: the larger church, the greater community prestige, the seniority of ordination, the nomination to committees that *really* matter, the gravitation toward urban core or suburbs, the return of couples you married years ago to baptize their children today. The more loyal the clergy are to the denomination and the denominational publishing house, the more the denomination rewards them by resolving their congregational conflicts and by providing off-the-shelf resources so they don't have to think too hard.

I am sarcastic, I know. But I have seen too many good people who happen to be clergy insidiously drawn into the career path, and all they really get is a modest pension, a secret handshake, and a heart attack. The lure of Jerusalem is so subtle and so destructive. There is immense safety in it—and almost no real joy. There is stability, but little creativity. There is collegiality, but little trust. There is theological certainty, but little existential integrity. There is happiness, but little ecstasy. Most of all, there is the insidious comfort of being among people you like for the sake of the gospel, but no passion to be among people you dislike for the sake of the gospel.

This is the lure of Jerusalem. This is the failed strategic plan of Acts 1–8. Hunker down in the "upper room," that one unchanging rock in a chaotic world, that oasis of peace in the grinding routine. Ask people to adapt themselves to your schedule and lifestyle. Invite the micro-cultures *inside* and call it "inclusivity."

Deploy the minorities (youth, women, people of color) to greet at the door and serve the meals. And celebrate "blended contemporary worship" that will powerfully motivate people to go home to lunch. Deploy the apostles to visit room-to-room and placate the best givers. Promote Ananias and Sapphira to the board of trustees, and treat Lydia, Priscilla, and Aquila with caution. Maybe they can lead the youth group.

The trouble is that clergy who are truly faithful in their heart, and who have not really forgotten the original missional passion of their calling, cannot endure the boredom or the entrapment. It's not overwork that brings on the heart attack. It's chronic unfaithfulness.

E-mail #18
Subject: Peter's Nervous Breakdown

Dear Christian Pilgrim:
Yes, you are right. Ananias and Sapphira were *not* appointed to the board of trustees. Peter killed them instead. Oh yes, if you want to split hairs, Peter merely rebuked them for holding back their money as a means of controlling the mission of the church to suit their personal interests, and the Holy Spirit killed them. You are also right that the Jerusalem Council in Acts 15 did *not* proscribe the gentile mission, but simply imposed certain executive limitations on their activities.

The reason all this was possible was because Peter was experiencing an extended nervous breakdown. The lure of Jerusalem was ever strongest in this apostle, and it took a mighty wrench of the heart to take him out of Jerusalem on the road to mission.

• Once he recognizes Jesus as the Christ, his first inclination is to build a house for him and guard the entrance. Jesus rebukes him as Satan for trying to hem him in.
• Peter objects to other people healing in Jesus' name because they aren't a part of the party or polity of the

group. Jesus rebukes the seventy and argues about seniority.
- He's the only one to take up arms on Jesus' behalf, and
the first to run away to the sanctuary of the upper room.
Jesus just stares at him as the cock crows.
- Even when he knows Jesus has been raised, he retreats
to the seaside looking for comfort. Jesus questions him
three times about his priorities.

In the end, God has to speak to him not once but *three times* on
the rooftop in Joppa. The tablecloth comes down and God yells
in his ear that God can declare *all* cultural forms clean, and *all*
micro-cultures eligible for the Gospel. And to drive the point
home, Peter is kidnapped by a cohort of his worst enemies,
hauled off to Caesarea to meet Cornelius, a despised Roman, and
the Holy Spirit is poured out on the gentiles *even before they have
been properly baptized* or graduated from catechism class.

Freed at last from self-destructive habits he chronically denied,
Peter kills the controllers, intercedes on behalf of the mission to
the gentiles, and leaves Jerusalem to hit the open road of mission.

E-mail #19
Subject: The Clergy Killers

Dear Christian Pilgrim:

I see that you are disturbed by the violence of the gospel. You
write: "I object to the style of your writing! This is the church we
are talking about, not some aberrant theological mafia! You imply
that Peter was a murderer, Ananias and Sapphira were evil, and
their death was an execution. In truth, Ananias and Sapphira just
felt really guilty, probably had weak hearts, and Peter felt really,
really badly about it all."

Do you see how already you are lured by Jerusalem? Already
you have embedded in you the seeds of your own future heart
attack thirty-five years off! Scripture does not say Ananias and
Sapphira were in poor health, nor that they were simply guilty of

failure to tithe. And there is no hint that Peter felt sorry for them. This is all the retrospective of Christendom, for whom the church is always nice, occasionally misinformed, and constantly in need of caregiving.

I assure you, the church is a place of violence. There is a spiritual warfare unfolding in the church, and if you are unprepared for it you will not endure two years in ministry in the postmodern world. There are dysfunctional, co-dependent congregational veterans who will stop at nothing to build a firewall across the road to Emmaus to keep you hemmed inside Jerusalem. And there are dysfunctional, co-dependent judicatory veterans who will stop at nothing to help them.

I'm just being honest. Count the bodies and you will discover there are more mean, selfish, childish, growth-resisting people in the membership of any established church on a Sunday morning than collected in the average mall food court on a Saturday afternoon. And Pastor, it's up to YOU to do something about it! Another sermon obliquely aimed at Ananias or another pastoral visit to pray with Sapphira won't change anything. You have to deal with it, head-on, in the hallway.

In my books *Coaching Change* and *Fragile Hope,* I list the "hierarchy of control" that Ananias and Sapphira will follow to sabotage your spiritual leadership.

- Fiefdom: protection of turf
- Denial: refusal to admit the truth about community and culture
- Inflexibility: using procedure and polity to block mission
- Institutional dithering: ad hoc committees to delay action
- Denigration: deliberate slander of the leadership
- Hostage-taking: blackmailing the church with money or influence
- King-making: support for change provided it is shaped around a privileged few

You can read about all this elsewhere, but my point here is that today most churches move very quickly through the first four steps to get right to the denigration. You spiritual leadership will evoke anonymous death threats, slanderous accusations, lies about your spouse, and threats against your children, not from the community, but from the church membership. These are the post-Christendom times we are living in. Count on it.

E-mail #20
Subject: Killer Clergy

Dear Christian Pilgrim:
Peter's transformation from timid, co-dependent disciple hiding in the upper room into a dynamic, innovative apostle who would travel to Rome is a revelation of how to endure the ministry. Had he remained "in residence" (geographically and spiritually), the young Christian movement would have died and Peter would have had a heart attack feeling guilty about his unfaithfulness. Once he made up his mind to be "in motion," Peter knew Ananias and Sapphira would try to stop him, delay him, and, if necessary, kill him. I mean it! These controllers would deliberately break his marriage and send him into disability if that is what it took to protect the church as their private oasis from the cruel world. So Peter killed them instead.

I'm not saying Peter was a murderer. I'm saying he was mission-driven. He was going on the road to mission, and he was not about to let Ananias stop him or Sapphira distract him. He was a dragonslayer. He killed *control*. He stamped out *dysfunction*. He didn't gather the board to develop a five-year, incremental strategic plan to stamp out dysfunction. He just stamped it out before it could fester, multiply, and undermine the mission.

This is why I say that when it comes to enduring ministry, courage is more important than competence. You have to be courageous enough to confront control and dysfunction, even though you may feel guilty about it, or you may take some heat for it, or you may lost your job because of it.

145

E-mail #21
Subject: You Got It!

Dear Christian Pilgrim:
You write: "And why would I have the courage to risk that? Because I really, really want to be with Jesus on the road to mission. Right?"

Bingo! Jesus predicted Peter would die in such manner that his hands would be bound and he would be led away to a place he did not want to go. Legend has it that outside of Rome he saw Jesus headed into town, turned right around to follow him, and was crucified for his faithfulness. But in a last act of defiance against co-dependency, he *requested* that he be crucified *upside down*. I love that story of audacity and courage. It's as if Ananias and Sapphira finally caught up to him, probably used the denominational polity against him, and just as they were about to crucify him Peter takes the initiative again. By requesting to be crucified upside down, Peter was saying: "And put *that* in your pipe and smoke it!"

So if you ever get crucified by congregation, denomination, or whoever, be sure your last act is to be crucified *upside down*.

E-mail #22
Subject: The Scales of Justice

Dear Christian Pilgrim:
I have in my imagination an old-fashioned balance or scales used to measure weight. Most clergy enter ministry believing that, if they are faithful, God will ensure that the accumulation of evil that they experience will at least be balanced (if not overbalanced) by the accumulation of grace.

The accumulation of evil on one side of the balance can basically be reduced to two things: guilt and anger.

- The guilt accumulates because they are never skilled enough, smart enough, quick enough, or adequate

146

enough for mission. They know all too well the trail of mistakes and missed opportunities they have left behind. And they have a very high, perhaps unrealistic, sense of perfection.

- The anger accumulates because they are forever victims. The fact that the public takes advantage of them (pan- handlers, governments, fellow "professionals," and the average selfish seekers, et al.) is bad enough. It feels much worse because churchy people are forever taking advantage of them as well (weddings, funerals, judica- tories, Aunt Nelly with a hurting bunion, the average selfish parishioner, et al.).

In the old days of Christendom, this accumulation of guilt and anger could be "balanced" (if not "overbalanced") by perks: vacations, days off, higher salaries and medical benefits, recognition, prestige, cama- raderie at the judicatory annual meeting, and if not a free car at least a free subscription to a clergy magazine. As the perks perish, clergy expect God will somehow replenish the grace on the other side of the scale. When that does not happen, they feel betrayed.

That may sound rather petty to you now, starting out as you are in a path of ministry. But just wait! In twenty years you will look around and realize that your good friends from university have now far outdistanced you in income, security, and options. They're sending their kids to Harvard, and you can't afford to send your kid to the local community college. They have a nice house, and you have a ramshackle parsonage. They took a holi- day to Bermuda, and you started a holiday in Fargo and were called back for a funeral. It gets to you after a while.

E-mail #23
Subject: The Spiritual Balance

Dear Christian Pilgrim:
I know. I'm sorry. I deliberately poured cold water on you after your passionate outburst to be on the road to mission with Jesus.

I just wanted you to think about how dusty that road will be. It will be so dusty that the dust will stick in your throat and threaten to choke the life out of you.

The image of the scales is still in my mind. However, the accumulating guilt and anger you feel is not balanced by perks, but by a particular spiritual discipline. Medieval monks would have described this discipline as one of moderation, cooperation, poverty, chastity, and fidelity. The more you discipline yourself (i.e., submit in obedience to a higher power), the less accumulating guilt and anger control your life. I prefer to talk about "gut work," "mind work," and "soul work" as the key to bringing spiritual balance to your life.

> ✓ *Gut work:* This is the constant cross-examination of motives, confrontation of addictions, and struggle against manipulations. It never stops. Shed the tears, vocalize the anger, train the body, seek absolution, and sweat. It helps to work out with credible companions.
>
> ✓ *Mind work:* This is reflection, self-improvement, mental conditioning, and constant questioning after truth, purpose, goodness, mission, and beauty. It accelerates and decelerates in the ebb and flow of culture and spirit. It helps to be opportunistic.
>
> ✓ *Soul work:* This is about going beyond praying, to making your life the prayer and the prayer your life. It is about transparency to the Infinite, and vulnerability to the unpredictable and uncontrollable Holy. You enter the soul and change it. You enter the mind and transform it. It happens in *kairos* moments. It helps to place yourself in environments of risk and multisensory learning.

The gut work keeps the "unbalance" of accumulating guilt and anger from resulting in a breakdown of health. The mind work keeps the balance at least level between guilt/anger and grace/hope. But the soul work is what can tip the balance in favor of grace.

I find that clergy are best at mind work. Perhaps that is because the seminary has trained them that way. Without the gut work, however, their reflection and self-improvement quickly becomes "mind games" and self-deception. Therapy might be an answer, but gut work has more to do with disciplining one's unique human nature for holistic health: personal, relational, physical, emotional, and so on. Clergy are so often intelligent people, but not really healthy people.

The hardest and rarest self-discipline is soul work. Unless this happens, no amount of reflection or health will keep you from burning out, dropping out, or opting out. I meet a lot of clergy on the brink of disability who talk about their desert-like experience. They complain that they never have *kairos* moments anymore, no life-giving, inbreaking experience of the Holy.

Sure, there are periods when such dry spells are part of living. Often the real truth, however, is *kairos* has not happened because clergy do not have the courage to make themselves vulnerable enough or transparent enough to the Holy. After all, the Holy hurts! Who would willingly want to sear their lips, dislocate their hip, or change their name? If you want to see a burning bush, you've got to leave Egypt.

E-mail #24
Subject: The Three Choices

Dear Christian Pilgrim:
"Discernment is so hard, particularly when it is clouded by responsibility for my husband and family. When the scales are weighted toward pain (guilt, anger, or whatever), how will I know what to do?"

The depth and honesty revealed in your question is in fact the first step. The easiest things to do would be to reverse your guilt or anger and project it on the congregation or your companions on the mission journey. Make *them* feel guilty! Rip into *them* for behaving badly! Well, maybe that's what a disciple of Peter the Dragonslayer should do! But before you do, consider the three basic choices. When in pain, change churches, change the church, or change yourself.

The most common choice is to change churches. Move. Relocate. Seek a new call. Get reappointed by the bishop. Of course, doing this simply to escape pain is not a healthy or mission-driven motivation for moving, but we see this again and again. On the other hand, there certainly are healthy and mission-driven reasons to move. Paul left Ephesus to move on to Philippi. The lesser reasons for this might be that the mission now requires skills or networking that you cannot acquire or provide, and, knowing your limitations and not wanting to get in the way of mission growth, you move on and let another take your place.

The second most common choice is to change the church. Confront it, reinvent it, reshape it, and transform it. Reprioritize the budget, redeploy the assets, and reconfigure the staff. Of course, doing this simply to make the pain go away is not a good motivation. On the other hand, doing this to multiply mission or have greater impact to change lives and change society will lead you to adjust your tactics. I've written books about this.

The last choice is the hardest. Change yourself. I don't mean accommodating yourself to the wishes of others. I don't even mean "paying your dues" to the controllers and dysfunctional co-dependent parishioners so that you can spend the rest of your time being faithful. I mean face your addictions, resist manipulations, recover the original passion of your call, and build a new companionship of pilgrims to fulfill your destiny with Christ. Let go the safety nets. Cling to Jesus.

E-mail #25
Subject: What If the Pain Is Unbearable?

Dear Christian Pilgrim:
Your question is so poignant that I suspect you have someone in particular in mind? Maybe your own pastor? Do you think he is on the brink? Is he about to burn out, drop out, or opt out? I had a feeling that his very defensiveness about our correspon-

dence and anger about the changing motivation, methodology, and content of mission immersion might belie deeper angst.

If the pain is unbearable, then focus everything on the spiritual life and nothing else. This is the time to step aside from the church and return to the desert, the cave, the monastic retreat. Stop preaching, stop going to meetings, stop counseling or being counseled, stop taking continuing education courses, and stop talking. Get out of the manse, get out of the judicatory responsibilities, get out of the office, and get out of the routine. And for God's sake, do not get into denominational office, institutional chaplaincy, or campus ministry, because you will do even more damage to the poor saps that follow you!

Focus on the spiritual life. Go back to the monastery. This in itself is not for the fainthearted! You are not going to escape from the world. You are going so that you can devote all your energy to wrestle with the devil. Discipline yourself to the gut work, mind work, and soul work. Surrender yourself to the power of God. Win that victory, and you will be able to emerge, scarred but whole, ready to engage mission once again.

E-mail #26
Subject: How Will I Know When It's Time to Move On?

Dear Christian Pilgrim:
One of the most difficult things a pastor must do is discern when it is time to move on. There are no simple rules. It is always ambiguous. Ego, self-interest, and the unpredictability of the Holy Spirit all blur the discernment process.

Ego blurs discernment because we always overestimate our leadership abilities believing we have what it takes for every aspect of mission, or we always underestimate our leadership abilities, disbelieving we have hidden gifts yet to be tapped. You need credible companions to carry you beyond ego.

Self-interest blurs discernment because those "companions" themselves have agendas to fulfill and axes to grind. Whether it's a bishop, a board, a spouse, or even your best friends, their advice is tainted by the temptation to use you for their own purposes. You need serious prayer.

Yet the Holy Spirit blurs discernment because it is both prophetic and apocalyptic at the same time. The Spirit can reveal future results based on the trends of your ministry, but it can also take mission right out of your hands entirely and change your world and your ministry in an instant. You need simple courage.

The best way to discern if it is time to move on is to look to the mission field itself. If you have given several years of your best leadership to ministry in your primary mission field (i.e., census tract, zip code, or the average distance community people drive to work and shop), then do this. Set a timeline of about six months. Gather a discernment group of credible advisors. And in that time frame ask:

a) Have more adults inside and outside of the church become involved in serious spiritual growth disciplines? (The measurement of adult faith formation)

b) Have more micro-cultures in the primary mission field connected to the Christian mission of this church? (The measurement of mirroring demographic diversity)

c) Have more volunteers in our church become personally involved in mission outreach, hands-on, embedded in their weekly lifestyles? (The measurement of multiplying mission)

d) Is the world really any different because we existed in the last six months? (The measurement of positive personal and social change)

If the answer is "no," then it is time to move on—but first try to understand the reason why so that you will not repeat the same mistakes again. If the answer is "yes," then stay, even if people in authority want you to go and even if stress is high. You cannot abandon the growing missionary disciples or the public's coming to know Christ simply because you are in hot water.

E-mail #27
Subject: How Do I Know When It Is Time to Get Out of the Way?

Dear Christian Pilgrim:

You write: "But I don't like being in hot water!"

Then don't be a minister. Life today is a bubbling cauldron of spirituality, and the fire is being stoked simultaneously by culture and Spirit. You have fallen into the Christendom habit of referring in your heart of hearts to "my ministry" as you would refer to "my career," "my job," or "my work." It really is *God's* mission, and you are just the peon chosen to get involved in it. You did not choose it, but it chose you. You did not deserve the honor when it was given to you, and you will not deserve the pain when it is given to you. It's never been about you. It's about God's mission.

So I think the bigger, deeper question clergy need to ask is not "How do I know when it is time to move on?" but rather "How do I know when it is time to get out of the way?" The former question assumes it is all about me. The latter question assumes it is not about me at all, but about God's mission.

The most profound, but also most glib, answer to the question "How do I know when it is time to get out of the way?" is to say: always! Clergy are *always* in the way, and they must *always* get out of the way. The parent must get out of the way of the child, the teacher must get out of the way of the student, the apostle must get out of the way of the disciple. That is always the hardest thing to do, and the one thing that must be done. Unless Paul and Silas had left town (as stated in the last verse of Acts 16), Lydia would never have risen to lead the Philippians to have the most effective ministry in the ancient world.

There is a "hidden controller" in all of us. If after six months of serious discernment, you see that adults are not growing, publics are not connecting, mission is not multiplying, and the world isn't any different, then nine times out of ten the *real* problem is not that the clergy have failed to do something, but that the clergy have succeeded in doing everything. And they have done it very well, very professionally, and very effectively. And it is killing the church.

Leave town. Get out of the way. Step aside from the pulpit, the office, the committee chairmanship, the judicatory leadership, the Bible study lectern, and the strategic planning process. Take a sabbatical, go to Starbucks, visit with your spouse, play with your children, or start another church somewhere else. Yes, this might mean leaving your church at the very moment when everything is going well and life is good. But for God's sake and the mission, *get out of the way*!

Get your ego out of the way, your professionalism out of the way, your ideological agendas out of the way, your theological purity out of the way, and yes, even get your salary out of the way! The truth is that God's mission is bigger, broader, and more awesome than your ego, your skill set, your ideological perspective, and your theological certainty. Until you get out of the way, the Spirit cannot have free reign and others will be denied opportunity to participate in that awesome, creative, innovative Spirit.

Do you see the real problem here? The problem is not your inadequacy, but your adequacy. It is not your lack of ability, but your great ability. It is not your lack of professionalism, but your extraordinary competence. The very things that grew a church to a certain point now block a church from reaching the next level of mission. You won't get out of the way, and the people have grown dependent on your abilities and *they* won't let you get out of the way, so unless you take drastic action to remove yourself from the mission *then the Holy Spirit will deliberately and forcefully remove you from being in the way!* Does that seem mean of God? Shouldn't God reward the very faithful and good servant and leave him or her in place to enjoy the fruits of success? But you see, it was never about you. It was about God's mission.

E-mail #28
Subject: Reality Check

Dear Christian Pilgrim:
Earlier in our conversation I likened the postmodern learning process to that of the pre-literate pilgrims from Chaucer's *Tales*.

These pilgrims devised conversational ways to critique one another as they traveled the pilgrim path. I've incorporated some of these tools in my congregational mission assessment book *Facing Reality,* but leaders use them both to grow and to endure on the dangerous road ahead. Here is the leadership application.

You can see that I have taken the ancient discernment of "Seven Deadly Sins" and "Seven Lively Virtues" and created seven continuums of discernment. Imagine the pilgrims on the road—or imagine you and your traveling companions in ministry—conversationally critiquing one another. On a scale of 1 to 10, how trapped are you by the deadly sin or how energized are you by the lively virtue?

Deadly Sin	Lively Virtue
Pride: It's all about me, my church, my heritage	Faith: It's all about Christ, mission, and gospel
Covetousness: Things, security, and wealth	Charity: People, their future, giving life away
Lust: Abuse, dependency, slavery to agendas	Prudence: Respect, permission, freedom
Envy: Jealousy, blaming others, success	Hope: Surrender, constant learning, desire for God
Gluttony: Excess, control, and consumption	Temperance: Boundaries, priorities, and trust
Anger: Hurt, violence, twisted retribution	Justice: Healing, vindication, reconciliation
Sloth: Laziness, staff dependancy, refusal to grow	Fortitude: Energy, discipline, courage to grow

This self-corrective used by companions on the road to mission helps them be confident in their own integrity. No matter what happens, remaining loyal to this essential integrity helps you endure the trials and overcome the temptations ahead.

E-mail #29
Subject: Sustaining Grace

Dear Christian Pilgrim:
"Earlier you talked about '*kairos* moments' as part of the 'soul work' of the minister. I know the Holy is unpredictable, but is there a way to anticipate these moments or make them more accessible? I need all the help I can get here!"
Your question—and desperation—is understandable. The early pilgrims wondered this too. The late-Christendom church later institutionalized their self-discipline into liturgical sacraments. But you need to go beyond this to recover the original experience of grace each implies. Again, I apply these to congregational life in my book *Facing Reality,* but you can apply them to leadership:

✓ *Rebirth:* The ways you experience personal transformation in relationship to Christ. Remember your baptism and be thankful!

✓ *Covenant:* The ways you experience being chosen by God, and shape your lifestyle around Christ. Remember your participation in the body of Christ and be thankful!

✓ *Repentance:* The ways you accept criticism, and reprioritize your time and energy in obedience to Christ. Remember God's unconditional love and be thankful!

✓ *Communion:* The ways you experience union with God in a daily walk with Jesus. Remember the intimacy of Jesus and be thankful!

✓ *Loyal Intimacy:* The ways you prioritize fidelity in any intentionally covenanted companionship in Christ. Remember your marriage and be thankful!

✓   *Calling:* The ways you discern your destiny in God's plan and stake your security to accompany Christ into mission. Remember your heartburst and be thankful!
✓   *Acceptance:* The ways you receive ultimate accept-ance of all that you are, and look forward in hope to eter-nity. Remember the promise of paradise and be thankful!

Perhaps you may take comfort and courage in the liturgical reen-actment of these experiences of grace. But you would do well to go beyond this and begin to recognize these sacramental experi-ences in daily living.

E-mail #30
Subject: Life in the Spirit

Dear Christian Pilgrim:
My mentor wrote a great deal about "life in the Spirit" primarily as it related to communities of faith, but I find myself applying these insights to the Christian pilgrim in particular. "Life in the Spirit" is life lived at the intersection of the infinite and the finite. That intersection is both ideal (resulting from the consciousness of symbol systems pregnant with meaning) and experiential (result-ing from the impact of the Holy seizing upon symbols to render them portals of power). Life in the Spirit is a kind of gut/mind/soul continuum in which the pilgrim acts, rests, and meditates. Thus the monastic rule of work, reflection, and prayer is not a sacred tactic to be imitated legalistically, but a paradigm for holistic living.
All this time we have been talking about "calling" as if it were something separate from life in general and unique to a peculiar species of human being (i.e., Christians). But when you look at the seven experiences of grace (or seven sacraments) in the pre-vious e-mail, you suddenly realize that calling is in fact *the sixth* experience of grace and not the first. Without the first five expe-riences of grace, calling is improbable, or will be unrecognized or unfulfilled. Most traditional clergy I know have done just this. They have divorced themselves from the first five experiences of

grace, and so the sixth experience of grace becomes insipid, bitter, and deadly.

"Rebirth" is the most fundamental. If you would endure as a Christian minister—indeed, if you would find any enjoyment in Christian ministry at all—then the inevitable, necessary, and repeated experience of radical salvation is crucial. It is not the memory of baptism (well, perhaps "memory" in the way that the earliest classical Christians understood Plato, but not in the modern psychological sense of that word). It is the re-experiencing of that moment which, every time it is recaptured, escapes definition and must be experienced again. It is the *desire for Christ*.

"Covenant" is the partnership for mission, shared with Christ, but also shared with the companions of Christ on the pilgrim road. This is not about contractual arrangements involving service and pension, but about absolute trust or a lifetime bond of mutual support. It has more to do with medieval oaths of fealty than with institutional promises. It is the *desire to be with Jesus*.

"Repentance" and "communion" follow upon rebirth and covenant as a kind of perennial double meaning. Repentance is about resisting the constant temptation to make everything a matter of "me" rather than a matter of "God's mission" (the first deadly sin being pride). "Communion" is the mystical restoration of relationship with Jesus that gives hope for tomorrow. It is the *urgency to merge oneself in Jesus*.

"Loyal intimacy" as an experience of grace has long been trivialized as "marriage." I do not imply that the integrity and fidelity of your marriage is unimportant. It's just that intimacy, as it was understood in classical times and by ancient Christians, had less to do with marriage itself and more to do with the perfect honesty and trust pilgrims invested in their peers or companions. While it is true that a frequent reason clergy burn out, drop out, or opt out is due to a breakdown in fidelity to marriage, I think it is even more true that it is due to a breakdown in fidelity among the companions of Christ. Loyal intimacy is the *surrender to life with Jesus*.

Take away, undermine, or diminish any of these five experiences of grace, and calling turns to dust. Renew these five experiences of grace, and calling becomes fertile again and bears God's fruitful mission.

E-mail #31
Subject: Sweet Surrender

Dear Christian Pilgrim:
"Last night I went to what was described as a 'traditional worship service' and got a real shocker. We actually used part of the
old Wesleyan Watch Night Service that you quoted way back in
the beginnings of our correspondence, and I suddenly felt like a
crusader knight from medieval times keeping an all-night vigil
before shield, sword, and crucifix. These words blew me away: 'I
am no longer my own, but thine. Put me to what thou wilt, rank
me with whom thou wilt. Put me to doing, put me to suffering.
Let me be employed by thee or laid aside for thee. . . . Let me be
full, let me be empty. Let me have all things, let me have nothing.
I freely and heartily yield all things to thy pleasure and disposal.'"

If most of the people who harp away at maintaining tradition
could just experience the real power behind the tradition they are
trying to maintain, they would not want the tradition. It would be
too hot to handle. It would be too awesome. Whether Wesley knew
it or not, these words and this spirit of surrender stand completely
in the spirit of the Desert Fathers and the early monastic movement.
Your image of the crusader is appropriate because it was monastic
preaching that launched the crusades, and the covenant of the crusader was borrowed from the covenant of the monastic novice.

Wesley's big mistake (or perhaps I should say, that of Wesley's
followers) was that he applied this sweet surrender primarily to
clergy, when in fact the original monastic intention was to apply
this to any and all Christians. Modernity's big mistake has been to
allow tradition to stand in the place of the infinite import that
seizes upon tradition as one among many vehicles of grace.

Yet all that is moot before your personal experience of "sweet
surrender." The adjective "sweet" refers to the sense of taste.
Surrender is not something you really ever understand, nor can
you ever fully describe it to others in words. It is not something
you just see and appreciate. Nor is it something you just touch
and use. It might be an aroma that you smell, but usually it is an

experience of ingesting God straight into your metabolism. It tastes good, doesn't it?

E-mail #32
Subject: Eternal Abundant Life

Dear Christian Pilgrim:

How will you endure this mission to the end? The covenant of the Watch Night Service you experienced ends with these words: "And now, O glorious and blessed God ... thou art mine, and I am thine. So be it. And the covenant which I have made on earth, let it be ratified in heaven." These last words are not mere rhetoric, nor dogmatic assumption, nor good poetry. These are words of real hope.

One of the tragedies of Christendom is that it reduced the significance of eternal, abundant life to an afterlife destination for elite people. It didn't take scientific, skeptical modernity long to then dismiss eternal, abundant life as a silly, unverifiable superstition advocated by hypocrites who really didn't deserve it in the first place.

Yet there is a reason why early pilgrims were preoccupied by eternal abundant life. They believed in a different kind of paradise for which they were willing to sell, risk, and change everything. Dante's *Divine Comedy* should be on your reading list. Guided by Virgil and Beatrice, Dante sees unspeakable evil and endures incredible suffering, but is sustained because he really does believe that eternal unity with God is worth it.

Paul often spoke of eternal, abundant life, not as a destination for the elite but as an experience of confidence. "We are always confident," he says, "for we walk by faith, not by sight" (2 Corinthians 5:6-7). He goes on to recount the afflictions, hardships, beatings, calamities, labors, and sleepless nights, and how the apostles were mistreated as impostors, scapegoats, and nobodies. "We are treated ... as dying, and see—we are alive." Now is the acceptable time. *Now* is the day of salvation. Not tomorrow or next week or upon retirement (2 Corinthians 6:2-10).

I realize that eternal, abundant life is not verifiable, but most things worthwhile in life are never verifiable. I also realize that you absolutely do not deserve eternal, abundant life anyway. I deserve it even less than you do. And yet that is the surprise of it! To be given the prize before the race even starts, so that you don't have to work for it, but just have to celebrate it! To be given a jovially divine promise that "There's more where that came from!" so that you don't have to hoard life, but you can just give it all away with reckless abandon!

E-mail #33
Subject: What Will the Future Really Hold for My Denomination, God's Mission, and Me?

Dear Christian Pilgrim:
The story of the earliest church, once again, reveals both the warning and promise God gives to the postmodern future. Read Acts 18, and there it is.

Throughout his early journeys recorded in Acts, Paul has had an ambivalent relationship with his parent religious institution. He has tried his best to reconcile the emerging mission to the gentiles with the infinite import that lay behind the traditions. Then, in a dramatic moment in the Corinthian synagogue (the traditional ecclesiastical institution of his time), his sense of rejection comes to a head. Scripture says he literally moves next door to the home of the gentile, God-fearing Titius Justus to carry out the mission.

This shift "next door" is a profound and symbolic action. It represents the final divide between the body of Christ in residence and the body of Christ in motion, a break between the parent ecclesiastical institution and the emerging postmodern mission, which will widen quickly as time goes by. The ambivalent relationship will continue, but not for long. When Titus Caesar and all the might of contemporary culture finally conquer Jerusalem, the parent ecclesiastical institution perishes. The body of Christ in residence disappears from history. I see this as a story that could *potentially* be reenacted in our time. In your time. In the next twenty-five years.

Perhaps it will not happen. Perhaps the parent ecclesiastical organization will not reject the postmodern mission to the spiritually yearning and institutionally alienated public today. Perhaps the best, brightest, and most mission-driven Christian leaders will not drop out or opt out of the denominational structures and seminary centers of higher education to "go next door" and set up entrepreneurial alternatives for the descendants of Titius Justus. I am working to prevent that from happening, but I am working hardest of all for the mission to multiply whether or not that happens. Even Scripture says that Crispus, an official of the traditional ecclesiastical institution, followed Paul "next door"!

But what about you? Will you be able to stay connected with the denomination and seminary, and will you sustain a relationship with your traditional ecclesiastical parent *and* pursue the mission to which you are called? Or will you end up "going next door"? Whatever happens, I urge you to ponder in your heart the vision Paul received on that fateful day in Corinth (Acts 18:9). The Lord Jesus said, "Do not be afraid, but speak and do not be silent; for I am with you, and no one will lay a hand on you to harm you, for there are many in this city who are my people."

So do not be afraid, and do not be silent. God is with you for abundant, eternal life. And whatever your experience of the institutional church, there are more people in North America than you can imagine who are God's people.

THE DRAMA OF THE PRESENTATION

BY LINNEA NILSEN CAPSHAW

"That's my story, you just shared my story!" a woman called to me as I walked through the lobby of a church after Tom and I presented Mission Mover to Convergence participants through a dialogue he had written in the form of an e-mail conversation. Then another woman chimed in, "And it's my story too ... unbelievable! I now feel legitimate in my ministry and mission work!"

I smiled and felt a deep sense of thankfulness that I had participated in a presentation that allowed some people to relate so fully to the story and understand for the first time that their ministry and call was worthy, even though they weren't following the traditional path to seminary and pastoring a congregation. And I felt deeply grateful to God for allowing me to walk a path that was similar in many ways, and different in other ways, to the woman in the e-mail conversation Tom and I had just presented. I, too, became a mission mover in a nontraditional way and could relate to the freedom these women felt when they realized their mission was just as important to God's work on earth as is the work of professionally trained clergy.

When Tom first asked me to participate in the presentation of this e-mail dialogue for his keynote address at EBA's 2003 Convergences, I was thrilled! Then I received the dialogue from him, read it, and wondered what people's responses would be. I feared some might roll their eyes, shut out the conversation, leave the room, and/or ask for their money back! So, I was pleasantly surprised when we presented at three different Convergence sites around the country in 2003 and most of the people stayed and listened! In fact, many seemed truly engaged in the conversation, trying to hear and absorb it all. And some related to every word and finally felt supported in their ministry efforts to follow Jesus!

As we planned our verbal presentation, Tom told me to go ahead and ad lib throughout the conversation, expounding on the feelings behind the words, adding conversations along the way that this woman might have had with God. With this goal in mind, I began to read the dialogue in preparation for our presentation and it came to life for me. My life was embedded in this woman's life in many ways. For instance:

Confused Christian said, "I was the one to ask you during the break whether you thought ordination was important or not for someone thinking about the ministry."

I'll never forget one of the conversations my classmates and I had as I was sitting in a final graduate school class for my hospital and health administration degree. The professor asked us to reflect on why we decided to become health care administrators. The responses from people ranged from, "My dad was a hospital administrator," to "You make a lot of money these days in this profession." When I chimed in with my response, "Because I want to serve others," most of my classmates looked at me like I had two heads. Making money was the predominant reason that my classmates had spent two years of their lives obtaining a master's degree. I was pretty stunned. I grew up in a Lutheran Christian tradition with the theology of the priesthood of all believers. I understood that I was called to live a holy life and to serve others, doing ministry in all areas of my life—in my career, my community, my household, in all I do. So I believed I could choose to be anything and choose to live that job as ministry in Christ's name. I initially chose hospital administration as a way to live out my ministry in my career.

I gained a wonderful education from this master's program for my ministry in the world. I learned about administration of organizations, big and small; leadership development; system analysis and development; team formation and coaching; living by mission, vision and values; and many other things. All of this education and experience has also been vital to my jobs in hospitals and to my call in ministry. By the time I was in the midst of my career as a hospital administrator, all of my siblings had started their lives in ministry—ordained ministry. It was at this time that I began to realize the difference between life in the ministry and life in ministry. I knew that I had been living a life of ministry in my job, in my service to others in the community and at church, with my family and friends. However, I reached a point in my life before I turned 30 when I was burned out in my ministry as a hospital administrator. After I hit rock bottom, I felt God spoke to me through the book *Halftime* by Bob Buford to respond to a call to live life in ministry to the church, using my gifts and passion to help build God's kingdom on earth through working with the leadership in churches.

This change of life caused me to then wonder, "Do I need to go to the seminary as my siblings had?" I was not being called to be a scholar in religion. I was not being called to teach religion. I was being called to work with church leadership to transform congregations and people's lives to live out the kingdom of God on earth. I had an education and experience in leading organizations and people to effectively live out their missions. Did I also have to go to seminary?

I cannot recall the number of times people have asked me when I, too, would go to the seminary. As I began consulting with congregations, a number of people told me I would need to go to seminary so I would be respected by the clergy and congregations

I worked with. I kept asking God if that was what I was supposed to do, and I kept hearing back, "No." I had the basic training I needed to live out my call with Jesus in mission, and the Spirit has led me to many different ways to enhance my education since then.

Then, after listening to Tom talk about all the frustrations of ministry, Confused Christian said, "You make it sound like ministry is a pain and all my friends are right to say I'm nuts to even think about it."

I recalled a time when I was a hospital administrator and so tired of all of the politics between doctors, administrators, board members, etc. I called my dad that night and was bemoaning working with these people and out of frustration I blurted, "Maybe I'll quit my job and become a pastor so I don't have to deal with these politics anymore." And he lovingly said, "Honey, don't fool yourself into thinking there are not politics in churches." I guess I never really understood all that my father went through as a pastor when I was growing up. We saw some of the strife and struggle; however, I do not have memories of a lot of politics being played, or maybe I just didn't see those games. Somehow I still thought that ministry in the church would be less of a pain than working in a hospital. Somehow I hoped it would be better since the focus of many churches is to help people live faithful lives. However, I have realized that it's many of the same people who are in the world, working at hospitals, who show up in churches and work on their committees. Whatever is causing people to act ugly in their hospital job can cause them to act ugly in a congregation. I

> After the presentation, some were angry that we questioned the need for seminary training and ordination into the ministry. Others were dumbfounded.

was not going to escape the pain of people's bad behavior by entering congregational ministry.

Confused Christian then stated, "But that's what I want to do: really be with Jesus! Why would I experience that as a pain? I think it would be sheer pleasure!"

I could imagine this person's struggle before she asked Tom this question again. She must have gone to God in prayer to ask, "Lord, how could being with you and your people be such a pain? Does he know what he's talking about? I know Jesus said that we would struggle in this world as followers of him, but I've never thought of that as being a pain."

As I was struggling with whether or not to quit my job and follow Jesus somehow, somewhere in mission, I asked God many times what that journey would be like. Was my father right? Would I find a lot of politics and haggling in the church just as I had seen as a health care administrator? Would Christian people in the church really tear each other down, backstab and manipulate others, doing hurtful things in the name of good? Would people be as self-centered and worldly in the church as in hospitals?

Although there was a time in my life when I liked to believe there wouldn't be frustrations in the ministry, I realized fairly quickly that I was mistaken. All I had to do was to read stories from the book of Acts or any of Paul's epistles to discover what it meant to be continually frustrated by people and circumstances, but also to be with wounders, people who can inflict deep pain on you. There are always frustrations when trying to accomplish things by working with others, when attempting to deal with people whose goals and timelines are different from yours, when working within the constraints of modern-day rules and regulations.

In addition, life can be painful whatever you are doing in this world. People are nice to your face one moment and stab you in the back another. People discriminate against you or others for any number of reasons. And sometimes people purposefully wrong you. I have experienced many situations that were a frustrating pain in the neck and also I have had times in my life in which I have been deeply wounded. I know I carried that pain with me to the congregations, work, and friendships I was involved in at that time. Ministry certainly doesn't shield you from pain of any kind. I know that. I just wanted to believe otherwise.

And if you're going to really be with Jesus in mission, it will be a big pain in the neck in more ways than you can imagine. The world often doesn't understand or want to have anything to do with you. Many people in the congregations I have worked with haven't wanted to hear about following Jesus in mission. They've been happy with their institutional Christianity. If you have felt the call of Jesus to move out in mission, then you need to know that you will put your basic sense of security and trust on the line over and over and over again. As I have discovered, following Jesus on the road to mission is not always easy, but it is worth it! The joys and freedom and hope and peace I have experienced since beginning this adventure are greater than any of the pains I've experienced along the way, and there have been many. But it is worth it!

During debriefing sessions at the Convergence, many people shared how they could relate to the experience of ministry being a pain, in a variety of ways. Others were frustrated that we were even talking about ministry as a pain; they hadn't experienced it that way at all. Again, people come from different experiences in life and we must respect that on our journeys.

Confused Christian then referred to her call to ministry as a career change, to which Tom replied that call is different from a career change, that call to church leadership in this day and age requires that you be wildly desirous to be with Jesus in mission.

This again brought back memories for me of my call process. I was a successful hospital administrator at a major teaching hospital in downtown Philadelphia, Pennsylvania. By the world's standards, I had it all at age 29: a high-powered job, a row house in center city, dinners out regularly, frequent travel, friends, family, and enough money to do whatever I wanted in life. But I was unhappy with my work because I felt pressured to do things that went against my values. And then, I was keeping myself so busy that I didn't have to face the fact that I had become burned out, totally empty inside. I'll never forget the evening that I was lying on my roommate's couch, sobbing uncontrollably, totally depressed, lost in life, wondering if I would ever find joy again. I was finally experiencing enough pain in my own life that I was open to listening to where God wanted me to follow Jesus with my life. I finally understood that if I got a job at another hospital or somewhere else, I would be making a career change and would probably be back to this empty position soon after taking a new job. Thankfully, God was calling me to do something different, and it was far more than a career change.

God called me intensely over a period of nine months to a place of freedom to follow Jesus in mission, no matter what the cost. I knew without a doubt that I was supposed to begin using my gifts to help build God's kingdom on earth. Granted, before this time I had been on many church committees and contributed to congregations and the community, but this was a call to be so much more, to use all that I am in mission—wherever the Spirit leads. It was time for me to leave my career goals and my job and respond with a "Yes" to God's call in my life.

> The women who spoke with me after the presentation knew exactly what this meant; call was not a career change, but a new way of being with Jesus that was exciting, wild, and scary at the same time. Others didn't appear to get it; they hadn't been touched that way ... yet!

Finally Confused Christian started to understand what Tom was saying, and she made the transition to a Companion of Christ in this conversation. She said, "I want to share the gospel as welcome relief. And I really want to multiply disciples and model a spiritual life that plumbs the depths of Christ! Wow! Oh, by the way, I said this to my friend who owns a Mail Boxes Etc. franchise, and she offered me a job. What's going on here?"

Similar to this woman in the e-mail presentation, I had friends who thought I was nuts! They couldn't understand how I could give up my career, give up the money, give up the lifestyle and prestige, to start my own business to consult with health care organizations and work with churches and faith-based organizations. They thought I should go take some time off, that I was too stressed by work, that I just needed a break. However, I knew that I could never go back, that no break would help me, that I was about to start the most exciting adventure of my life and I had no idea where it would take me. I was also confused, scared, and unsure about this move, wondering where it would lead.But I knew I must go because I was nuts—nuts for Jesus and the freedom I had been given to follow him in mission! I knew that my life had been transformed by God, from a place of emptiness to a place of hope and I wanted to share that with others. I didn't know how, when, where, what, or with whom, but I did know why I needed to follow this call. Jesus had changed my life and I wanted to help others experience the same transformation in their lives. That was enough knowledge for me at the time; the rest I left up to faith and trust in a loving God.

I could tell there were people at the Convergence also who thought Tom and I were nuts to have presented what we did. Some of them said it with words, others with facial expressions, a few with their feet. And that was okay ... I had already experienced that in my own personal life, so I understood people would react differently to this presentation as well. We are all at different places in our lives and God will work with us just where we are. I know, because God responded that way with me!

"So Tom, are you saying that denominational certification and seminary training are irrelevant for contemporary Christian mission?" Companion of Christ inquired.

Wow, was I so encouraged to read Tom's response to this question:

"Not irrelevant, but secondary. Seminaries and denominations that were once major players in the training and deployment of ministers are now minor players in the training and deployment of mission movers. They are useful to teach some subjects, train some skills, and broker some networks, but are no longer dominant partners."

After having many people tell me that I would need that seminary certification and/or training in order to be a "legitimate coach/consultant" with congregations, it was freeing to hear that it's not the only way of training for people moving forward with Jesus in mission. I didn't have to feel guilty about not going to get a divinity degree anymore. I could feel free to take classes that interested me and/or would help me out in the phase of mission I'm in, but I didn't have to spend years in the seminary system just to be legitimate. Amen and Alleluia is what I felt when I read this!

However, after the presentation, a number of people at the Convergences shared with me that they couldn't believe that basic seminary training wasn't *essential* to being in the ministry today. I can understand their struggle. However, we need to allow options. We need to let people go to learning opportunities appropriate for their growth, and not bind them to an established model of training. And we need to encourage those who have been trained by seminaries to continue their learning along the journey.

Companion of Christ then asked the question many of us have asked: "I feel totally inadequate to do it, to be in mission with Jesus. What do I do? Where do I go?"

Fortunately, when I first started my business to coach and consult with churches, I was lucky enough to talk directly with Bob

Buford, author of *Halftime* (the book God used to change my life) and founder of Leadership Network. I shared with Bob the work I had been doing with physicians and their staff to empower them in teams to use their gifts most effectively to provide high quality patient care. Most physicians were trained in technical medical skills, yet doctors were spending the majority of their time in the office doing work they weren't trained or called to do. I shared with Bob how I thought pastors ended up in the same situation, trained technically in theology or pastoral care, and then having to do a million things they weren't trained or called to do. I wanted to help pastors, staff, and lay leaders live out who they were called to be to lead congregations. I needed help in translating what I had been doing in health care to the church.

Bob then explained to me how the world was changing and roles were changing in the church, and that seminaries were probably not the best place for me to go to receive the type of training I was looking for. I would be better off reading books, taking seminars from some of the leaders in church consulting in the country, talking to people in the field. Bob was sharing with me the strategy for mission movers that Tom has articulated in this conversation.

And so my journey began. The first nontraditional learning experience I had regarding the church was at the Changing Church conference held by Prince of Peace Lutheran Church in Burnsville, Minnesota. Carol Childress from Leadership Network was one of the speakers and after she finished, my dad and siblings who were at the conference with me said, "So this is what you've been trying to tell us about how you can work with churches to help them achieve mission. Now we get it!" Then the Holy Spirit just seemed to take me under its wings and lead me to partnerships and learning experiences that were right for each stage of mission I have been in during these eight years. Whether it was learning to assess, equip, or coach congregations, the Spirit led me to incredible opportunities and partners in mission. In addition, learning and partnerships opened up for me related to the church's role in supporting people's call in the world, and in supporting women in church leadership. And my story of partnerships goes on and on. . . .

I have been so blessed by the Spirit's guidance for my mission! It took me time and growth in my spiritual life and disciplines to learn how to listen for and hear the Spirit's nudges, a never-ending process on the journey. However, I learned that I didn't need a seminary to give me the kinds of partners in mission and learning experiences that I've had on my road to mission with Jesus. These partnerships, led by the Holy Spirit, have impacted my life and ministry more than I could ever describe. What a blessed way to learn and grow!

> "I have been so blessed to have people to walk, struggle, rejoice, and share life with on this journey in mission," she said.

"So, were do I find a mentor and a team?" Christian Companion asked when she began to understand the idea of partnership Tom was suggesting.

These were some of my questions when I first read Tom's recommendation to find a mentor and a team: And what if I find many mentors along the journey? Is that okay? And what if my mentor isn't a Christian? Is that okay? And what if I find team members whom I need to communicate with "virtually"? Is that okay? And what if the team members change along the road to mission? Is that okay?

I have been amazed over the years at how God used the most unlikely people to mentor me along the way. When I was a hospital administrator, I worked with two separate consulting firms to accomplish various work at the hospital. Both firm representatives became mentors to me and I didn't even realize it. When I started working with them, I had no idea that I would be starting my own consulting business within two years. Yet, as I began to feel the call to leave my career job and start my own business, I was able to confide in and ask both people any question that I had about the process, such as how to be most effective as a consultant and coach, how to deal with travel around the country, and many more questions. They had both modeled in different ways what it was to be a high impact consultant.

I watched, I learned, I asked, I learned, I shared, I learned. They connected me with people I needed to know along the way. One of them gave me the opportunity to partner with him in health care consulting, which helped give me a sense of security that allowed me to take the risk and leave my job. In the end, the partnership didn't amount to anything because our values were different, but through the hope of that potential relationship I gained the courage to take the significant risk to start my own business. I thank God for those mentors in my life, people who did not profess a strong Christian faith yet guided me to respond to God's call.

I have been fortunate enough to have had many mentors along the journey who also have the same core values and beliefs as I do, mentors who have not only connected me with other people on the journey, but also, more importantly, have guided me on my spiritual journey and helped me holistically balance ministry, family, and God priorities in my life. I am so thankful for their guidance and openness over the years and look forward to many more.

Not only have I experienced the blessing of many mentors along the way that, frankly, I feel I did not seek out but the Holy Spirit brought to me, but also I have had the opportunity to work on teams with a variety of people. Again, as the Spirit has moved me to new places on the road to mission with Jesus, I have had the blessing of many teams. When I started my own business, I often feared that it would be a lonely adventure. What I quickly realized, both in health care and working with congregations and faith-based communities, is that there are many people like me in business for themselves who are willing to come together as a team when necessary to meet a client's needs. We often come together in mission for Jesus, based on our shared values and beliefs. We share not just our ministry, but also our journeys in life. We support each other during life challenges and celebrate the great joys that occur. We laugh and cry together, pray together, eat and drink together, and walk with each other. Without team members, I would feel so incredibly alone on this road, for it is not an easy walk. We all need fellow sojourners along the way. It is a blessing to have team members in my life!

In conversations at the Convergence, many didn't understand how a mentor and team could substitute for good seminary education; and many could see how that would work. The secular world has been emphasizing the importance of mentors and coaches in people's lives for a long time—the church is catching up! In the secular world, organizations have focused on building teams to fulfill mission for decades—the church is catching up! So many people understand and appreciate from their jobs and community service the concepts of mentors and teams; however, because much of the education for church leadership has not focused on that concept recently, it has become a difficult transition for others to make.

And then Christian Companion stated, "Personally, I really feel a need for some fundamental education in scripture, history, theology, and missiology. I hate to admit it, but what I don't know would fill volumes!"

I fortunately learned quickly that for the mission work I would do with congregations—work in organizational and staffing development, leadership, volunteer empowerment, mission and vision development—my hospital administration graduate degree studies would be extremely useful. My work does not require that I have a significant education in scripture, history, theology, and missiology, and so I didn't feel pressured to obtain that type of education. Maybe it also was because I grew up as a pastor's kid, went to a Christian college, minored in religion and learned a significant amount along the way, maybe it was because my mother was always trying to help us experience learning in new ways at home, or maybe it was because I knew Jesus had transformed my life and that was all that really mattered, but I didn't worry very much about a fundamental education from a seminary. Whatever the reason was, I am glad I spent my time learning from books, conferences on topics of interest, online seminars, the Internet, and other such learning opportunities as I needed them. Just-in-time learning has been such a part of my journey. When I learn something, I apply it, and it sticks! That's just who I am. And I suspect that there are many others like me. Certainly, there have been times when I have felt that I didn't know enough about a particular issue to do my work most effectively. However, when that happens, I stop, do research, and find out what I need to know before I move forward in mission.

One of the women I talked with after a session said, "I like the seminary classes I have been taking and I think I'll continue to take ones that interest me or would be useful in my current ministry. What was so freeing about the presentation you made was that now I don't feel like I HAVE to finish a seminary degree and become ordained to live out my call in mission. It's a choice now for me, not a necessity, and that is so freeing!" And that's right on target. When people understand that there are options to learning how to be in mission as a church leader, they are free to choose the path that works best for them.

"And you are saying that what he calls training for 'practical ministry' is unimportant?" Christian Companion stated. And Tom replied, "Practical ministry training is crucial, but it is more crucial that you are prepared to equip others with your training than for you to do all the ministry you've been trained to do by yourself."

I'll never forget going to my first Leadership Training Network five-day seminar on equipping people for ministry. I went within a year of leaving my job as a hospital administrator, and I finished the training saying to myself, "What is new about that? In health care administration, we've been equipping and empowering employees to work on teams based on their gifts to develop ideas that fit within our mission, vision and values for years."

The fact of the matter is that, as Tom stated, pastors are called to equip people for ministry in the world, not to do it all! In so many places in the Bible it talks about how we're all gifted as members of the body of Christ, and are called to use those gifts to serve others in the world. So if we're all gifted, then why do so many congregational members ask the pastor to do the entire ministry? The expectation for many clergy, both from their seminary training and from their congregations, is that they function as "little gods," and many clergy have ended up burned out as a result. Thankfully, there have been significant movements within the church to recognize that we are all part of the body of Christ and that pastors are called to equip people for service. There are many examples of congregations that have been transformed and are helping people find their roles in the body of Christ and live them out in their whole lives.

Again, it was Bob Buford's book *Halftime* that helped me first see that I could use my spiritual gifts of leadership, administration, and faith to help build God's kingdom without being a pastor in a church. It was the Leadership Training Network that helped me see that I could use those same gifts to serve congregations that desired to equip people for ministry without being a pastor. It was one of the EBA team members who helped me realize that I really am functioning as a pastor, outside of the traditional definition of pastor, because my coaching and consulting is focused on equipping pastors and non-pastors to discover and live out their calls from God in the world. I did resist that labeling for a time; however, the Spirit convicted me that I was serving in a pastor's role as described in Ephesians 4 and that I needed to continue to equip pastors of congregations to serve as equippers themselves.

My brother, who is a pastor at a large Lutheran church in Ohio, shared that recently he received a letter, through his bishop, from a member of his church stating "her church just wasn't Lutheran anymore . . . because all the pastors ever do is train people for ministry." My brother rejoiced; it was finally sinking in that he and other pastors weren't going to do all the ministry of the church. They were getting through to people. He was thrilled, yet she was frustrated. It's time for more congregations to hear the Spirit's call to equip people for ministry and life in this crazy world!

"My husband has a question. He asks, 'When will it end? When will you graduate? When will your career effectively begin?' And while he is a Christian, and supports my call to ministry, he wants to have some predictability and stability in our lives. What will I tell him?"

When I heard my call to follow Jesus in mission, it was an easier decision for me because I wasn't married. Although I was dating Dan, I didn't have children, I didn't own a house, I really had nothing to hold me back. I always knew I could go back and work in health care administration again if things didn't work out, so although there was a level of risk for me, it wasn't the level that many people experience. I have learned, however, that no matter what your circumstances are, if you respond to God's call, God will make your call and journey possible within your life situation.

Since I heard my call, I married Dan, who knew me briefly as a hospital administrator before I left that job. I thought Dan would be thrilled that I was working and making money by consulting, coaching, and training with a variety of congregations and nonprofits around the country. However, periodically I would moan about getting on plane after plane for work and Dan would quickly respond, "Well, you're the one who wanted to be the international woman consultant! Maybe you should think about getting a full-time job locally so we can have predictability in our lives, so you don't have to leave me all the time, so you can make a regular income." Yet at the same time, Dan has always said, "I am here to support you wherever you're called to ministry." It has been a struggle for us during these eight years to journey through the unpredictability of this Jesus walk. And it has been a great joy to follow Jesus! What a challenge it has been to "plan for the future" when we know what's most important is that I follow my call, wherever that leads us.

However, God in God's mercy has shown faithfulness time and time again by walking with us on this journey. Dan and I both trust God so much more after eight years of this unpredictability than we ever had previously. We have seen what we hope to be the hand of God protecting us, guiding us, leading us, showing us a new way to live that results in us experiencing the kingdom of

God here and now. We are trying to do our part to be faithful to God as well, sharing with others the love, joy, peace, hope, and life abundant that we experience so that they too may know the kingdom of God here and now. Being with Jesus and experiencing the kingdom is more important for us than predictability, stability, and getting a career job in town. And so we journey on together. . . .

Recently, one of my partners in ministry shared how her husband just wouldn't understand her call to ministry in this way. For a variety of reasons, they are separated from their marriage at this time and do not know where it will end. However, she, for the first time in her adult life, feels free to do what she needs to in order to respond to her call. She trusts that God will be with her and support her and make her whole, no matter how her marriage ends. She is trying to be faithful to her call from God, and in that, she has had to make very difficult decisions. For a time, she felt darkness; now she feels the light of Christ leading her and trusts there is hope on that road with Jesus in mission!

"I wonder how joining a pilgrim band is going to help me lead a church in rural North Dakota, urban Philadelphia, or remote Newfoundland," said Confused Christian!

I think if I had been told over eight years ago that I would need a pilgrim band to journey with me on this road to mission, I would have wondered the same way Confused Christian did. What is Tom talking about? What is a pilgrim band? Is it the same thing as other groups?

Tom said, "Unite with a companionship of travelers, much like Paul traveled with Silas, Luke, Priscilla, Lydia, Timothy, and Onesimus. Separately or together, wherever you go, whatever you do, this is your primary support group for prayer, critique, planning, and support. Share the stories of life struggle and spiritual victory with your companions along the way."

Little did I know that eight years after responding "Yes" to God's call, God would bring together for me a pilgrim band, a group locally that is on the same journey to follow Jesus, struggling with similar issues, rejoicing in the transformation in their lives that Jesus has brought, and asking similar questions about the role of church leadership in this day and age. I had a bit of a relationship with each of these people individually, but didn't know any of them very well. Through classes at the Servant Leadership School of the Church of the Savior, two of us heard that it was time for us to have an accountability group in our lives. And so we ventured out to ask two others if they were interested in forming a group. Within a few weeks, we had our first gathering.

Although our original intent was to hold each other accountable for spiritual growth and whole life ministry, what the Spirit has led this group to be for me is so much more. It has become a pilgrim band that is on a journey similar to mine. Our times together have allowed us to be fully open and honest, supporting each other, challenging when necessary, and always praying for one another. I gather with each one of them individually at various times to continue the conversations and do some ministry together. I know my pilgrim band would be there for me in whatever I was going through and challenge me to always listen to God's will for my life. Now I understand the need for a pilgrim band and the joys experienced together!

One of the members of the group I just described was an attendee at a Convergence. Since the Convergence, he has continued to refer to how thankful he is for our pilgrim band in his life. As a pastor, he is struggling with significant issues right now with his denomination about where and how his current congregation is called to be on the road in mission with Jesus. As can be expected, he is finding significant resistance both from within the congregation he leads and from outside the congregation through the denomination. He is not sure that he will be working for a denomination within the next few years, because many around him don't understand his vision and mission and don't want to change from the way things have been done in the church. He can't imagine walking through this process without his pilgrim band. He has gained courage to speak the truth in love and, when the church forces are working against him, he receives encouragement and support through prayer and hope in conversations with his pilgrim band. He has also been challenged by our pilgrim band members to determine if it is really Jesus he is following in this decision or his own ego. For now, he is staying on the road in mission with Jesus, whether it works within his denomination or not—that's the power of a pilgrim band!

"So Tom, can you paint a picture of how people like me can get on with Christ's mission with integrity?" Christian Companion said after becoming more excited and confused about how to equip herself than ever before.

As I think about this woman's desire to get on with Christ's mission with integrity, along with so many others who desire the same thing, I realize that there is not one answer to her question. All Tom and I and others can share with you are our experiences of being called to mission with Jesus. Your experience will be different. Once you say "Yes" to the call, then it is so important to trust God on the daily and future journey. Allow that trust to grow over time. Trust is so hard for us as humans, for we often experience people breaking trust with us. Can God really be different? I have learned through my experience that God is always faithful and will provide. Hard times will come, suffering will happen, disappointments will occur, yet God will be there through others to pick you up, comfort you, support you, and encourage you. And through that, you will grow in faith and trust of God on the road in mission with Jesus.

As you are faithful on the road, as you listen to where God is calling and leading, the Spirit will surprise you when you least expect it. You will meet people who are just right for you at a certain time in life, doors will open for opportunities that you didn't know about or think were possible, windows will shut that you were sure were ones you were to go through and then you'll find out later it was a blessing that the window shut. When you let the Spirit lead, you will be amazed at how things happen in your life that you never could have planned or predicted. When the Spirit guides, you will be open to anything that you and others confirm the Spirit is leading you to. You may move to places you never would have expected to live. You may live a married or single life, opposite of what you had planned for your life. You may quit or start a ministry role that seems well beyond your areas of giftedness. You may give more and more of your income to serve others in life, wondering how you could still live so well on the money you have left. You may lead others to places they never would have gone in the past, or gone alone.

Through these examples and many more, you will experience the grace of God time and again. Grace that allows you to do so much more than you are able on your own. Grace that allows you to be free to follow Jesus. Grace that allows you to walk through the dark times in life with trust that light will come again. Grace that allows you to forgive others as you are forgiven on the journey. Grace that allows you to experience more love and joy in your life than you can ever imagine. Grace upon grace upon grace. That's what it is like to walk with Jesus in mission as a church leader today. Step out boldly. Cherish the Spirit. Enjoy the journey.

On Getting Left Behind

I have never liked the phrase "retreat center." Christians don't "retreat." They "advance." That's why I refuse to do "retreats," although I love to be a part of "advances" and am building a decentralized model of what I call an "advance center."

But your church doesn't have to advance and go "forward." It can retreat and go "backward" just as easily as "forward" in its inner and outer unfoldments. The history of civilization is littered with stories of societies that underwent "moral" decline in their history. Nature is full of organisms that failed to adapt and descended into obsolescence and senescence.

Nothing can remain the same. There is no "pause" button for the church. As Tom Bandy has so powerfully portrayed in *Mission Mover*, there is only one way to resist entropy: move "forward" in mission or move "backward" into irrelevance. Too often the church has become entropy made visible.

How did we arrive at this place where, as one theologian admits, "most if not all current institutional versions of Christianity have failed in one way or another to provide a meaningful framework for the spiritual life"?[1] How did we arrive at the place where, in the words of one Christian leader, "because Christians are largely irrelevant, if there's a life-changing message to present, we'll make it boring and put it in a context you're not involved in"?[2]

As soon as your church decides to advance and become a "mission mover," you can count on the "We can't leave people behind" conversation. It manifests itself in other phrases as well: "Where's the compassion?" or "We've got to make sure everyone's on board." Or the real clincher, "Jesus didn't leave anyone behind."

Really?

Martin Luther didn't leave people behind? John Wesley didn't leave people behind? Rosa Parks didn't leave people behind? When she moved to the front of the bus, she left her friends behind. Any leader who doesn't leave some people behind never "moves." In fact, leaders are by definition people who leave people behind.

"But Jesus didn't leave people behind."

Really?

Even on the cross between two thieves, Jesus had to leave one behind. Jesus comes and gets us, but we decide whether to go with him or get left behind.

Original Sin is another name for Original Choice. One of the better themes of the Harry Potter series is the reminder that people are responsible for the choices they make, which makes it all the more important to make responsible choices. Many choices masquerade as "freedom" but are really bondage. We love our idols, and God respects our loves, our choices.

It is truly a matter of Truth or Consequences. Churches choose every day whom they will serve. A leader's task is to present as best we can the truth. The church's task is to decide. And there comes a time when leaders must honor the decision. Jesus even gave us a sacrament of failure for the ritual of leaving behind: "shake the dust off your feet," Jesus said, and try again.

I'd still be pastoring a church in the Genesee Valley (New York) if my "first-love" church hadn't decided, after quadrupling in size in five years, that it was tired of moving forward and wanted to settle in and stay in place. "We've come so far in so short a time," many of them said to me. "Don't keep pushing us. Leave us alone for a while."

So I did.

Leonard Sweet
Drew University
George Fox Theological Seminary
preachingplus.com

---

1. Nicholas Capaldi, "What is Bioethics Without Christianity," *Christian Bioethics* 5 (Number 3, 1999): 246-62, 247.

2. David Bruce, founder of HollywoodJesus.com, a website geared to exploring pop culture from a spiritual point of view. Quoted in Donald F. G. Hailson, "The Sanctified Soak: Cultural Engagement Evangelism," *Journal of the Academy for Evangelism* 17 (2001-2002): 70.